Small Moments,
Strong Bonds

Small Moments, Strong Bonds

LANA JOHNSTON

First published in 2025 by Lana Johnston

© Lana Johnston 2025
The moral rights of the author have been asserted

All rights reserved. Except as permitted under the *Australian Copyright Act 1968* (for example, a fair dealing for the purposes of study, research, criticism or review), no part of this book may be reproduced, stored in a retrieval system, communicated or transmitted in any form or by any means without prior written permission. No part of this book may be used or reproduced in any manner for the purpose of training artificial intelligence technologies or systems.

All inquiries should be made to the author.

A catalogue entry for this book is available from the National Library of Australia.

ISBN: 978-1-923225-94-7

Book production and text design by Publish Central
Cover design by Julia Kuris
Illustrations by Kim Langsdorf

The paper this book is printed on is certified as environmentally friendly.

Disclaimer: The material in this publication is of the nature of general comment only, and does not represent professional advice. It is not intended to provide specific guidance for particular circumstances and it should not be relied on as the basis for any decision to take action or not take action on any matter which it covers. Readers should obtain professional advice where appropriate, before making any such decision. To the maximum extent permitted by law, the author and publisher disclaim all responsibility and liability to any person, arising directly or indirectly from any person taking or not taking action based on the information in this publication.

CONTENTS

Preface	It's not too late	vii
Chapter one	Creating meaningful connection	1
Chapter two	Finding the gaps	23
Chapter three	Lightening your load	39
Chapter four	Balancing your head and heart	51
Chapter five	Creating a care squad	63
Chapter six	Your connection choices	77
Chapter seven	Creating intergenerational connections	91
Chapter eight	Mastering connection	107
Conclusion	The seeds of tomorrow's memories	125

Preface

IT'S NOT TOO LATE

Do you remember the last time you truly connected with your ageing parent or loved one? Not just checking if they've taken their medication or helping with groceries, but really *connecting* – sharing stories and laughing together, or simply being present in each other's company. These moments of genuine connection are often buried under an avalanche of practical tasks – racing between work meetings and doctor's appointments, juggling family commitments with medication schedules and coordinating care services. Every day feels like a marathon, and you're sprinting just to keep up.

Like many others caring for ageing loved ones, you probably find yourself caught in a cycle of *doing* rather than *being*. The urgent crowds out the important. Those deeper conversations you've been meaning to have are postponed. Again. The family stories you want to capture remain untold. The simple joy of spending unhurried time together becomes increasingly elusive.

This book exists because I know we can do better.

Meaningful connection with your ageing loved one is possible, even amid life's seemingly endless demands. It's not about cramming more onto your already full plate – it's about weaving connection into the fabric of your daily interactions.

Drawing from my personal life and professional experience in the corporate world, I've developed practical strategies that work in the real world. Time is always tight. Emotions can run high. But as a people and culture expert, coach, and connection specialist, I've seen how simple changes in approach can transform relationships and create lasting memories. Creating meaningful connections doesn't require massive amounts of time or energy. It requires intention and understanding of how to make small moments matter.

In these pages, you'll discover:

- the importance of connection
- how to create meaningful moments in just minutes
- practical tools to break through emotional barriers

- methods to help you balance practical care with emotional connection
- strategies to reduce future regrets
- simple techniques to make every interaction count.

This isn't just another book about caring for ageing loved ones. It's about reimagining connection in ways that fit real life. You'll learn how to move beyond task-focused interactions to create moments that matter, without adding more to your already busy day.

You'll find many enlightening examples throughout the book. These are taken from my personal and professional experience. Some of them are from friends, some are from clients, some are from colleagues, and some are my own.

When you look back on this time …

I understand because I've been there. Watching my dad's battle with cancer and seeing each of us race into action, I realised too late how many opportunities for meaningful connection we'd missed while focusing on the tactical aspects of care. The solutions I share are designed for people like you who want to do right by their loved ones and struggle to find the time and energy for meaningful connection.

Most importantly, this book is about hope. Hope that you can create meaningful moments of connection, even in challenging circumstances. Hope that you can find joy in your relationship with your ageing loved one, even as roles and dynamics change. Hope that when you look back on this time, you'll feel peace knowing you made the moments count.

"The questions we wish we'd asked become the regrets we carry. Start asking them today."

As we begin this journey together, remember it's never too late to strengthen your connection with an ageing loved one. Small changes consistently applied can transform your relationship in ways you might never have imagined.

Let's discover how.

Chapter one

CREATING MEANINGFUL CONNECTION

Caring for an ageing loved one

Everyone deserves memorable moments. Memories are a rich resource you and those you love can draw on to brighten and lighten the tougher parts of life, like when you get older.

For those in your life who are ageing – your parents, aunts or uncles, or just a friend in their last years – you may feel two conflicting needs:

1. a sense of urgency to build a treasure trove of memories before your ageing loved one dies
2. a growing list of tasks your ageing loved one needs your help with that distracts you from spending memorable moments together.

This book is about restoring the balance in favour of wonderful memories and meaningful connections. I'll show you how – and why – you must distinguish between two aspects of caring for an ageing loved one: the *deliberate* and the *tactical* connection. And then I'll share ways to get that balance right – despite all the pressures in your life, and the sense you probably have that you are already doing your best and you want no more pressure on your to-do list. I hear you. But I've got some clever solutions.

The two types of connection

I see two main types of connection happen between carers and their loved ones: *deliberate* and *tactical*. These apply to all the people you care for – children, colleagues and so forth – but here I am talking specifically about your ageing loved one. Getting clear about the difference between these two types of connection is at the core of this book.

Both are important, but they are different, so I will start by explaining what these terms mean.

Deliberate connection

Being deliberate is at the heart of meaningful connection. I love these two words: deliberate connection. Connection creates a sense of joy and self-worth for us all. We don't need the researchers to tell us this (although they do).

Deliberate connection is an intentional, meaningful interaction that goes beyond day-to-day, transactional tasks. It's about creating memorable moments amid the chaos of life – quality time that builds lasting memories and deepens your relationships. It is about creating moments to connect with your ageing loved one with deliberate intention. When you do so, you create memorable moments, which are easy to identify because they resonate long after they occur. These moments strengthen your bonds with others, bring joy to you both, and transcend time. They create stories that you'll cherish, share and reflect on for years. They will bring a smile to your face when you are climbing into bed or a bath after a long day, or prompt a warm exchange with others as you reminisce.

Memorable moments are not about giving expensive gifts or going on exotic holidays. Those might be fun, although this isn't where those moments usually occur. Instead, you will find them in your everyday interactions with others when you apply the power of intention. It can be as simple as:

- a shared laugh over a cup of tea
- a conversation about a long-forgotten but treasured photograph
- giving your undivided attention to your loved one
- engaging in meaningful conversations
- planning and sharing activities
- creating moments of joy, laughter or reflection together

- actively listening and responding to their thoughts and feelings
- showing physical affection when appropriate, such as holding hands or hugging.

Tactical connection

Deliberate connection sounds ideal, doesn't it? But for many of us, the opposite is much more common. We feel rushed, frustrated and, at times, resentful as we try to meet the needs of those we care about. Why? Because in most cases, those of us caring for ageing loved ones are part of the sandwich generation, which means we are stuck in the middle of a lot of demands – the meat in the sandwich. We have children at home, a partner, ageing parents or other loved ones, not to mention a career and perhaps a burgeoning Pandora's box of middle-aged health issues creeping up on us.

The sandwich generation

When you're a member of the sandwich generation, facing numerous competing priorities, your time is consumed with tactical actions – the parent–teacher meeting, sorting pills into the pill box, making that important work presentation, let alone trying to squeeze in a trip to the gym.

In this chapter, and this book, I am real about this kind of difficulty. As a 'sandwich' woman myself, I know the challenges we face, and I have coached many clients with similar problems over the decades.

Tactical actions are the necessary, time-consuming tasks that come with all caring roles. They are the practical, tedious responsibilities of life. Admin, bills, insurance and emails – not just for you but increasingly for your ageing loved one. Checking and double-checking. Popping in to see them and popping out to get them the stuff they need. You probably feel more like a personal assistant than a son, a daughter or a grandchild – always focused on the next appointment or medication time.

The core struggle we sandwich-generation carers face is the tension, guilt, frustration and even shame that we feel between fulfilling these practical duties and creating meaningful connections.

My Dad first battled cancer in his sixties, emerging victorious after an aggressive fight. When it returned, Mum thought he was just tired from golf. By the time we received the diagnosis, he had little time left. In those last months, we all fell into roles. Everything became a blur. Mum became the organiser. My sister and I helped wherever we could.

Looking back, we all became very tactical – doing what had to be done.

Then, for two beautiful weeks, his brothers, other family and some friends visited from Ireland, England, Hong Kong and various parts of Australia. They filled our grieving house with chatter, laughter, drinks and music. Dad was in his element, his Irish spirit buoyed by these wonderful moments.

The doctors told us to prepare for his passing in the new year. Life had other plans. Dad left us on 15 December with my sister playing violin by his bedside. I arrived too late. Even though we had a handful of beautiful moments, I felt keenly that we didn't have enough of them. We ran out of time.

In the months that followed, as well as experiencing intense grief, I felt a deep sense of regret at the missed opportunities for connection.

Rebalancing your connection

Many might argue that tactical actions help your loved one and show you care – they are a connection. And yes, practical care is a powerful expression of love and commitment. And, depending on how you do those tasks, they can offer ways to genuinely connect.

But be honest with yourself – how often are you simply running in and out, bustling your ageing loved one into and out of the car, the house, the doctor's surgery? It's crucial to distinguish between care tasks and genuine connection. How long is it since you have just laughed with, shared stories with or enjoyed the company of your ageing loved one rather than doing paperwork and errands?

By rebalancing your connection deliberately, you can make sure your practical care duties don't overshadow opportunities for deeper connection. This change starts when you recognise the difference. Only then can you create space for both. Yes, your loved one needs your practical support, but they also need your presence, attention and emotional engagement. Balance creates a fulfilling care relationship.[1]

Does this sound good to you, or does it sound like I am oblivious to the demands you face in your life? Perhaps you are wondering if I am a true representative of the sandwich generation or if I have a secret support network making my life easier. (Spoiler alert – I do, but I'll show you how to get one, too.) Believe me, when I was caring for my dad, I felt utterly sandwiched, so no judgement here. I am on your team.

What does the research say?

After my dad's death, I realised there is a lot of research about the various types of connection, impacts on wellbeing and the role of carers. Throughout this book I refer to Australian studies because I live here, but I've also checked international resources and there seems to be little difference in the results. The national peak body representing carers here, Carers Australia, published a 2024 report that offers relevant statistics. For example, carers

---

[1] And don't stress. I will show you how you can make it fun and get your sh*t done, too. The ideas in this book will help you with all your relationships, including those at work, so look forward to being a looser, more chilled-out sandwich person in future – more of a gourmet salad sandwich than pressed Devon.

"Connection regrets are the largest category in the deep structure of human regret."

Daniel Pink

make up 12% of the Australian population, and their wellbeing has declined. They were more than twice as likely to have low levels of wellbeing compared to the average Australian adult. There is an emotional toll and time pressure that carers experience, and you are not the only one whose time is consumed with tactical actions.

It's not just me who recognises the value of connection and considers the needs and desires of our ageing loved ones. There has been extensive consultation within the aged care industry, and changes to the national Aged Care Standards came into effect on 1 July 2025. These reforms represent a fundamental shift in approach, placing the aged care consumer at the centre of the model. The strengthened standards acknowledge what many of us have known intuitively – that quality of life for older Australians depends not just on clinical care but on maintaining meaningful connections and honouring individual preferences and dignity. This legislative change reflects growing recognition that our ageing loved ones need more than just practical assistance. They need to be seen, heard and valued as individuals with unique histories, preferences and contributions to make.

The Harvard Study of Adult Development, an 85-year longitudinal study, found that nurturing meaningful relationships is a critical determinant of happiness and overall wellbeing. Two of the researchers, Robert Waldinger, MD, and Marc Schulz, Ph.D., wrote a book called *The Good Life*. It emphasises that connection reduces feelings of isolation, promotes mental health and mitigates risks associated with loneliness and social isolation.

The weight of regret

Regret is a heavy burden. It can be all-consuming and destructive. It's evolved that way to act as a guide. When we do something we regret, we feel bad, heavy and burdened. The next time we face a similar choice about what to do, we remember that regret and (hopefully) don't make the same mistake. Learning from our mistakes gives us the power to improve the future.

You will regret it if you don't create memorable moments with your ageing loved one. This is a truth that you need to hear (and you are not the only one – most of us need to hear this). Your connection with your ageing loved one must be deliberate, meaning you have considered how to make it feel good for both parties. If you don't connect deliberately, you underestimate the regret that is coming your way. And that goes for all ageing loved ones, including parents who have let us down badly.[2]

One of the most widely referenced books in this space is Bronnie Ware's *The Top Five Regrets of the Dying*, drawing from her work as a palliative care nurse. When palliative care workers ask people about their regrets at the end of life, two themes consistently emerge at the top:

1. wishing they'd had the courage to live a life true to themselves
2. wishing they'd spent more quality time with the people they love.

The power of this isn't in the statistics but in what it tells us about human connection. It reminds us that in our final moments, it's not our work achievements or material success

---

[2] Later, I'll share some strategies for handling conflicts and past hurts while keeping yourself safe.

that matter most – it's the relationships we nurture and the authentic connections we create.

This knowledge can help us make better choices today. While we're busy managing careers, raising children and handling daily responsibilities, we can still create meaningful moments with our ageing loved ones.

My experience with Dad taught me two big lessons:

1. Caring for a sick loved one is intense and draining.
2. If you miss the opportunities to connect, you *will* regret it.

I don't want you to struggle with the regret I feel about the everyday moments I could have cherished more, the conversations I could have had and the memories I could have created. For that reason, I'm passionate about helping you and others create meaningful connections before it's too late.

My experience with Dad changed the way I relate to Mum as she gets older. It's been fantastic how our relationship has deepened as I have learned more about deliberate connections and how to foster them. The ideas in this book have worked for me and for many others I have worked with.

The mutual benefits of deliberate connection

You and your ageing loved one will both benefit from more deliberate connections – and suffer without them. The effort you make benefits your loved one, and it benefits you.

These deliberate connections nurture the emotional bond between you and your ageing loved one. I noticed a big difference when I planned for quality time with my Mum over each school holiday period.

Deliberate connection acts as a powerful antidote to the stress, isolation and loss of identity often experienced on both sides of caregiving relationships.

By fostering deliberate connection, you can transform the caretaking tasks – which might be seen as a burden – into periods of growth and fun.

The mutual benefits

Here are some key benefits you will both experience.

Rediscovering your loved one

You may feel as though you are rediscovering your loved one as you shift the balance from tactical to deliberate. You might hear a familiar story with fresh ears or learn something new about their past. Such moments slow time down, allowing you to be present. They have the power to transform your feelings from regret into fulfilment. It isn't just about improving the life of your ageing loved one. It's about enriching your own life and those of future generations by strengthening these vital familial bonds.

We are addressing a profound human need by encouraging people to create these moments now. We're helping them avoid future regrets and live more fulfilling lives. For example, my friend Jodi discovered a new side of her father through their shared hobby of gardening in his final years. What began as a simple activity became a gateway to deeper connection, offering both physical and mental benefits. Together they would spend hours in the garden tending to plants – the physical activity providing gentle exercise for her father while the fresh air and sunshine lifted both their spirits. Their prized achievement

"We need to listen to our regrets! They are powerful emotional signals that give us agency to change things."

was the row of tomato plants that yielded impressively large, flavourful fruit.

The joy wasn't just in growing the tomatoes but in transforming them into their favourite shared meal. Those tomato-harvest dinners became cherished rituals where stories flowed as freely as the homemade pasta sauce.

This experience echoes what happened when my colleague Chris gave his mum a tomato plant. She planted it in the vegetable garden at her care facility and took great pride in nurturing it. When those tasty tomatoes appeared, they became a highlight in her day and a great talking point during visits and phone conversations.

By creating meaningful moments now, you're building memories that will sustain you long after they're gone while enriching both your lives in the present.

Creating meaningful moments when memory fades

For some of you, your loved one may not even recognise you most of the time. It can leave you wondering how you can benefit from deliberate connection when they don't even know who you are.

I am not an expert in dementia, but I know from those around me that connection is equally important for those with dementia. Emotional connections persist even when cognitive function declines. Your loved one may respond to your presence, touch and tone of voice – even if they don't recognise you.

For those whose ageing loved ones face memory challenges, the focus shifts. It's less about 'creating memorable moments' and more about 'meaningful moments' where you're simply being present together. People with advanced dementia often experience moments of clarity during calm, one-on-one interactions. Music is often a great way to get memories and positive emotions flowing, too. As Chris shared with me, sometimes the most profound connections happen in the simplest ways – like sitting with his mother listening to 'Winchester Cathedral', a song that brought back happier times for both of them. While she may not have remembered their interaction afterward, during those precious moments together they both felt a level of peace and joy.

You will get glimpses of the person you've known and reduce their anxiety and improve their mood at the same time. Try simple activities like looking at photos, listening to music or sitting quietly together. Pay attention to non-verbal cues for signs of positive connection. Your effort to connect provides comfort and honours your relationship regardless of cognitive state.

TAKE ACTION: AWARENESS

For the next week, track the time you spend with your ageing loved one and categorise activities as either 'tactical care' or 'moments of deliberate connection'. If it's tactical and task-oriented – doctor's visits, cleaning, shopping, transporting – put it in your tactical column. If you feel it's a memorable moment – a laugh, a movie, a walk, a nice lunch – put it in the 'deliberate connection' column.

At the end of the week, reflect on the balance. Are you surprised by the results? For now, just notice your current patterns of connection. Try not to judge yourself. You are doing the best you can right now with your time constraints.

This exercise might trigger a bit of guilt – just park that for now. We'll come back to this reflection later in the book. Just know that you have taken the first step towards deliberate connection with your ageing loved one. *Yay.*

TAKE ACTION: REFLECTION

This is an exercise to help you feel determined and inspired to create those moments. Reflect on whether regret increases your determination. For example, on a scale of one to five, with five being the highest, how determined are you to create a more deliberate connection with your ageing loved one?

If you are not at a five, what is holding you back? We've discussed time, but sometimes your concerns may run deeper. Perhaps you wonder if your ageing loved one really wants a deeper connection – they may not be the kind of person who expresses their emotions much.

Or perhaps you think, *I want to create these meaningful moments, but I'm afraid of saying or doing the wrong things. What if I bring up a sensitive topic and upset my loved one? It feels easier to stick to safe, routine conversations.*

We are going to address all of that as we move through the book. This isn't about imposing anything on anyone. It's about inviting, opening and exploring.

For now, connect with how determined you feel to make changes and notice what might stand in your way. Have a chat with your partner, another family member or a friend about this. They might shed light on feelings or ideas you haven't thought of.

TAKE ACTION: CONNECTION INVENTORY

Try the connection inventory. List 10 activities that make you feel truly connected to your ageing loved one. Keep these activities simple and everyday. Here are a few suggestions to get you started:

1. Share an afternoon refreshment or favourite snack.
2. Discuss a favourite book.
3. Look at a map together and share stories about places you have been to.

Now, share your list with your ageing loved one and talk about which of the activities work for both of you. Do they have any to add?

Keep the list handy, for example, at your ageing loved one's home. When you have a moment, refer to this list as a reminder of connection opportunities and agree on one that suits the time you have available.

John talked about how his Mum loved prawns, so when visiting he would bring baked bread rolls, fresh tiger prawns and soft avocado, then make up lunch. They would sit there eating them together and sometimes not even talking. It makes him smile, even now, thinking about it.

Remember, the goal is progress, not perfection. You might not be able to think of or agree on many activities to start. Be patient with yourself and your loved ones as you explore these new ways of connecting.

Small, intentional moments

In this chapter, you have learned that there are two kinds of connection: tactical and deliberate. The heart of connection is deliberateness. We've explored the struggles you face as a member of the sandwich generation and how hard it is to make time for deliberate connection. And you have also learned there is hope in the pages of this book.

Once you can recognise the difference between various types of connection – between *doing for* and *being with* your loved one – you will be on your way to creating small, intentional moments that will make a big difference to the quality of connection.

We've looked at the big reason for creating connection: to create memorable moments and avoid the weight of regret. This book offers many practical ways to foster connection despite the demands on your time.

Remember, at its core, caregiving is about relationships. By balancing the practical with the personal, you're not just providing care, you're preserving and even strengthening the bond

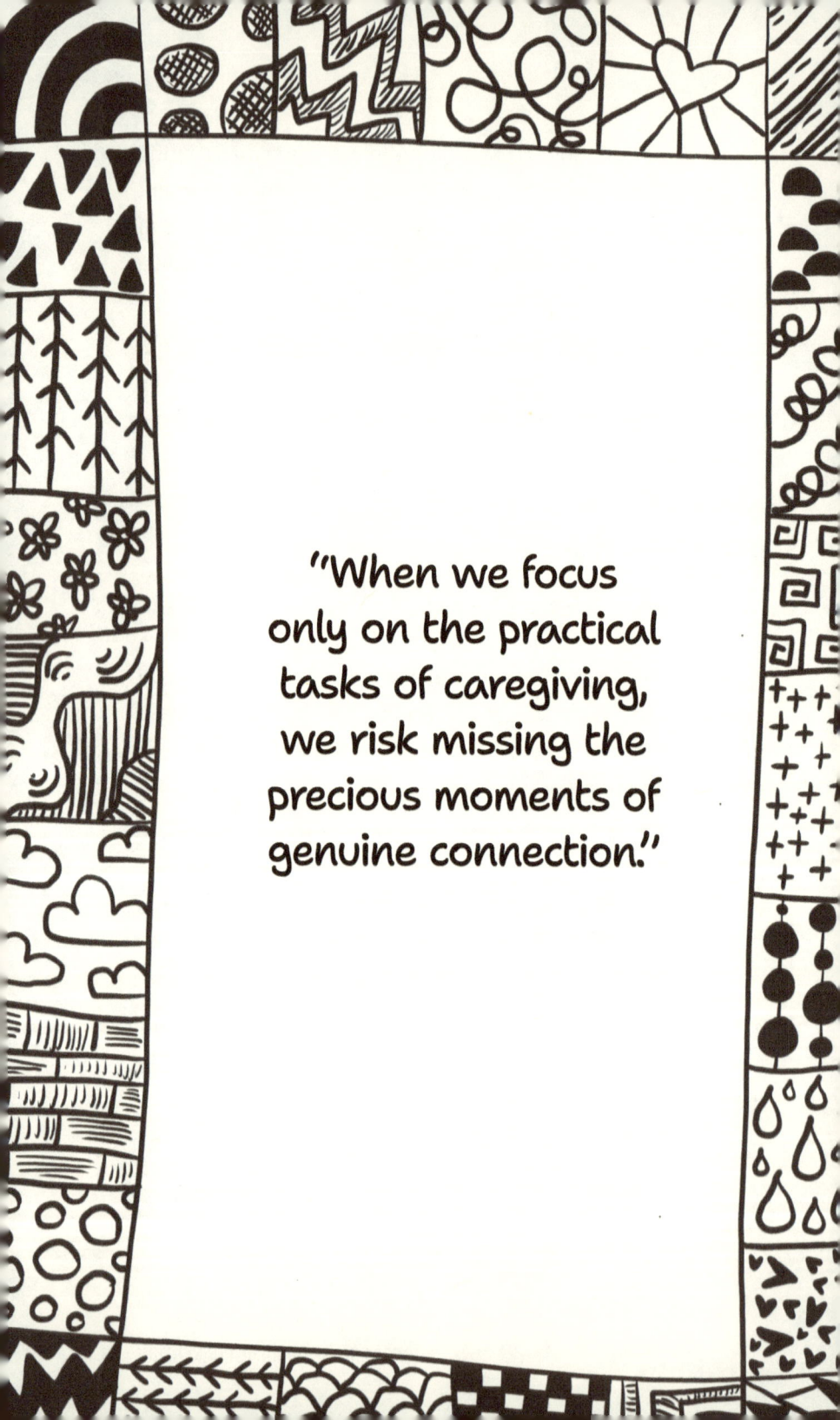

"When we focus only on the practical tasks of caregiving, we risk missing the precious moments of genuine connection."

you share with your loved one. This approach makes the carer journey more meaningful and fulfilling. You'll learn to stop prioritising tasks and busyness over intentional, meaningful moments of connection with your ageing loved one.

In the next chapter, I will show you how to revolutionise your relationship with your ageing loved one – one memorable moment at a time.

Get ready to embark on a transformative journey and uncover hidden opportunities for meaningful engagement. You'll discover powerful tools to assess your interactions and pinpoint exactly where you can create those unforgettable moments of connection. This is where the magic happens, so buckle up. You're about to take the first exciting step towards a more fulfilling, joy-filled relationship with your ageing loved one. Let's make every moment count.

Chapter two

FINDING THE GAPS

Understanding connection

Great connections don't happen by chance. They require a clear understanding of where you stand today and where you want to be in your relationship. Think about where the gaps are now that you want to fill.

Looking into the future is equally important – anticipate where new gaps might emerge. Ask yourself: is my loved one likely to become immobile in the next year? If so, what could that mean for our connection now and in the future? How might our interactions need to adapt if their health situation changes?

By considering potential future scenarios, you can strengthen your connection now in ways that will sustain you both through any coming changes. Perhaps it means prioritising certain activities now while they're still possible, or developing new shared interests that will remain accessible as physical abilities change.

Awareness forms a foundation

Take a step back to assess the current state of your relationship with your ageing loved one. Honestly evaluate the quality and frequency of your interactions. Identify areas where you feel disconnected or where communication breaks down.

Awareness forms a foundation for meaningful change. This is not a superficial checklist of activities or a one-size-fits-all approach to connecting with older adults. I'm talking about a thoughtful, personalised reflection on your unique relationship dynamics. Don't compare your situation to others or feel guilty about past shortcomings. Gain clarity on your specific challenges and opportunities for growth. This empowers you to take control of your relationship's future.

This process might feel like opening a door you've been hesitant to approach. It could involve hard conversations with yourself, asking truths you've avoided and shining a light on aspects of your relationship you've kept in the shadows.

In this chapter, we'll explore two crucial areas that will help you transform your relationship with your ageing loved one:

1. **Your personal connection assessment:** a self-reflection process to evaluate your current connection. This honest appraisal is your starting point for meaningful change. By articulating the current state of your relationship, you can identify strengths to build upon and areas that require attention.
2. **The SMILE framework:** a practical framework for enhancing your interactions. This model will help you imagine the positive changes that deliberate connection can bring, motivating you to act.

Through these, you'll gain the tools and insights to bridge the gap between your current relationship and the meaningful connection you desire with your ageing loved one.

Your personal connection assessment

Take an honest look at the quality and frequency of your interactions with your ageing loved one. Examine your communication patterns, shared activities and emotional closeness.

This is not a clinical evaluation or a standardised test. Don't compare your relationship to others or judge it against any idealised standard. This is a personal, introspective process tailored to your unique relationship. It's about gaining clarity on your specific situation, free from external pressures or expectations. This should be a thoughtful exploration of how you currently connect, what's working well, and where there's room for improvement.

This assessment is your gateway to changing the relationship for the better. You'll be asking yourself tough questions like, 'When was the last time we had a meaningful conversation?' Or, 'Do I really know what's important to them right now?' But this is your chance to build a legacy of love, not missed connections. Be crystal clear about whether the connection with your ageing loved one is where you want it to be. If it's not, after this assessment, you will know where to start.

This will also have benefits for you as a carer. When carers have their psychological needs satisfied – for example, relatedness and competence – their wellbeing improves, according to a 2023 study *Frontiers study on caregiving and relationships*. The study examined how adult children prepare for caregiving roles and how preparing impacts stress and relationships.

You might be thinking, *I already know my ageing loved one well. We've been family for decades. Why do I need to do an assessment?* Familiarity doesn't always equal understanding. As people age, their needs, interests and perspectives change. What mattered to your loved one a decade ago might not be what's important now. This assessment isn't about testing your knowledge of their past – it's about tuning into their present. It's a tool to help you spot subtle shifts you might have missed and identify new ways to connect meaningfully. By doing this assessment, you're committing to growing and deepening your relationship no matter how long you've known each other.

TAKE ACTION: RATING YOUR CONNECTION

Set aside five minutes of quiet time. Grab a pen and paper or open a notes app on your phone. Think about your ageing loved one – overall, how do you currently rate that connection from 1 to 10, with 10 being the strongest connection? Write down that rating.

Poor connection at a 1 could mean:

- totally avoiding conversations or having intimidating conversations

- the frequency and quality of communication between you and your ageing loved one isn't where you'd like it to be

- the depth of emotional connection is surface-level and transactional.

Strong connection at a 10 could mean:

- you are both committed to nurturing the relationship and have great examples of this
- you feel secure and protected in each other's presence
- you enjoy the mutual exchange of wisdom and knowledge – that intergenerational learning
- you know you genuinely care about each other's feelings and wellbeing.

You may decide that you'd like to increase this rating and therefore the number and quality of connected moments with your ageing loved one. What will it take to move your connection up just one point on this scale? Sometimes the most meaningful improvements come from simple, consistent actions.

Take my friend Sarah's experience. She established a standing lunch date with her father every second Tuesday. What began as a simple meal evolved into something much more significant. They chose the same café each time – a place that became 'their spot'. The predictable timing and location created a comfortable rhythm that her father could anticipate and look forward to.

Over time, these weren't just lunches but anchor points in both their lives. When her father began experiencing health challenges, these Tuesday meetings became even more precious – a constant in an otherwise uncertain time.

"It was never really about the food," Sarah said. "It was about creating a deliberate space, and that became a foundation for some of our most honest conversations."

What simple, regular commitment might you establish that could gently strengthen your connection?

> **TAKE ACTION: DESCRIBING YOUR CONNECTION**
>
> Take a moment to articulate the current state of your relationship with your ageing loved one. This involves honesty and assessing the frequency, quality and depth of your interactions, as well as the emotional landscape of your relationship. It might feel like writing a letter to yourself, detailing the highs and lows of your recent interactions.
>
> Describing your connection is about creating a clear and honest baseline. It's an essential step in identifying where you are so you can thoughtfully plan where you want to go in your relationship with your ageing loved one.
>
> What words would you use to describe the connection you have with your ageing loved one?
>
> Where do most of your descriptor words sit? On the left or on the right? What other words would you use?

Poor connection words could be:	Strong connection words could be:
Distant	Deep
Cold	Genuine
Disconnected	Solid
Superficial	Empathetic
Aloof	Supportive
Tense	Trusting
Awkward	Nurturing
Unengaged	Harmonious
Antagonistic	Meaningful
Strained	Resonant
Hostile	Synchronised
Disengaged	Committed
Disinterested	Bonded
Incompatible	Cohesive
Resentful	Affectionate
Fractured	Authentic
Unsympathetic	Aligned

Reflect on your answers. Do they reveal any patterns or opportunities for deeper connection? Maybe you don't feel that you really know each other well – that you don't appreciate each other's perspectives, especially if you have differences.

This exercise helps you become more aware of the quality of your interactions and identify specific areas for improvement.

Moving towards the right column isn't always easy. You might face resistance, both from yourself and your ageing loved one. Change can be uncomfortable. But setting the intention to shift even one aspect of your connection towards the right side of this table can create powerful momentum. Remember, this isn't about perfection. It's about progress. Even small movements towards deeper connection can transform your relationship over time. The goal isn't to suddenly jump from 'distant' to 'close' but perhaps to move to 'somewhat distant' as your first step.

You might struggle due to time constraints, emotional discomfort or difficulty remembering details. You may overthink the process, fail to see immediate benefits or face interruptions. You might even resist the potential changes this reflection highlights. These barriers can make introspection challenging, despite its long-term value.

If you struggle with this, start small. Set a five-minute timer and jot down the answers to the following questions about your last interaction with your loved one:

- What went well?
- What didn't?
- What's the one thing you'd change?

This bite-sized reflection can spark insight without overwhelming you. And remember – simply holding the intention to move towards deeper connection is the first and most critical step in this journey.

The power of assessment

Things will be clearer when you describe them in your own words. Self-assessment is more than just an exercise – it's a powerful tool for transformation. Even just the act of regular self-assessment can prompt behavioural changes, even without additional interventions.

By rating your connection and then describing it, you create a complete picture of where you stand today. The numbers give you a benchmark, while your descriptions reveal the emotional reality underneath.

When you document specific examples of interactions – both those that went well and those that didn't – you create a roadmap for change. These real-life scenarios become powerful motivation to continue what's working and adjust what isn't.

In my years working with organisations, I've seen how assessment creates the foundation for meaningful change. Without knowing where you truly stand, improvement becomes random rather than intentional.

You might struggle because you're not used to thinking this way. It may require an extra step of observation for a period. But the clarity you gain from honest assessment is the first step towards the deeper relationship you desire with your ageing loved one.

The SMILE framework

My SMILE framework helps transform everyday interactions into meaningful connection opportunities:

- **See the good and the needs.** Notice what's strong while staying attuned to what might be missing in your interactions with your ageing loved one.

- **Make moments memorable.** Bring lightness, presence and even playfulness into caregiving spaces, prioritising joy alongside function.

- **Intentionally connect.** Recognise that meaningful connection doesn't happen by accident but by design, showing up with presence rather than just proximity.

- **Listen deeply and lovingly.** Honour stories before solutions, creating space for shared narratives that bridge generations and build memory banks.

- **Embrace the 1% shift.** Focus on small, consistent actions rather than sweeping changes, understanding that tiny daily improvements compound into meaningful transformation.

This framework isn't about perfection – it's about progress. It's designed for real people with real time constraints who still want to create meaningful connections with their ageing loved ones.

The beauty of the SMILE framework is its flexibility – you can apply it during a five-minute phone call, while sorting medications or during longer visits. It shifts our focus from "doing for" to "being with" our ageing loved ones, which is where true connection flourishes.[3]

You might think, *I've tried things like this and they haven't worked*. But remember, there are infinite possibilities, and you might have aimed too high.

What have you tried already? What's working and what's not? What does significant look like for you? Describe who you wish to become when you think about the way you want to connect. Think about how to apply the SMILE framework model to a tactical activity. For example, with a trip to the doctor, you could turn the drive into a mini road trip with favourite music and conversation about favourite bands or singers.

Go for the 'one percenters'

Small changes create meaningful differences when connecting with your ageing loved one.

This approach is backed by science. The Big Joy Project, a research initiative by UC Berkeley and UC San Francisco, found that tiny intentional acts – called 'micro-acts' – improved people's emotional wellbeing by 26% and relationships by 30%.

---

3   I share lots of short-, medium- and longer-period ideas in chapter six.

Steven Bartlett, host of 'The Diary of a CEO' podcast, powerfully reinforces this concept through his work on incremental progress. Bartlett often discusses how monumental change rarely happens overnight; instead, it's the result of consistent small actions taken daily. He calls these the 16 steps that compound over time, creating profound shifts in our relationships and personal growth.

As Bartlett shares with his millions of listeners, "Success is the product of daily habits – not once-in-a-lifetime transformations." This philosophy applies perfectly to deepening connections with ageing loved ones. Each small moment of attention builds trust, creates memories and strengthens bonds in ways that occasional grand gestures cannot.

You might be thinking, *I'm overwhelmed. Every time I try to plan quality time, my to-do list takes over. What if I can't make the changes I want? What if factors beyond my control get in the way?*

This is where the 'one percenters' come in – tiny, manageable improvements that add up to significant change over time.

Think about making your relationship just 1% better each week. These small steps feel achievable and sustainable. Here are five simple one percenters you can start today:

- Send a morning text with an old photo of you both, asking, "Remember this day?" This takes 30 seconds but sparks joy and conversation.
- Put a reminder in your phone to call during their favourite TV show's ad break. Chat about the program they're watching.
- Write down one question each week you've always wanted to ask about their life. Keep it in your wallet or on your phone as a conversation starter.

- Create a shared music playlist of songs from their era. Add one song each week and listen together.
- Start a 'Sunday Story' tradition – ask them to share one childhood memory while you have your morning coffee. Record it on your phone.

Like the participants in the Big Joy Project, you'll likely find these small acts compound into meaningful improvements in your relationship and emotional wellbeing. Take Clara, who started having Sunday tea with her grandmother. She had noticed that her grandmother, who had become increasingly withdrawn at her aged-care facility, would dress up for these tea sessions. She'd put on her favourite blouse and even style her hair – something the staff mentioned she rarely did anymore. During these Sunday afternoons, Clara brought along a small photo album or an object from their shared past – her grandmother's old recipe book, a piece of jewellery with a story, or newspaper clippings from events that were significant to the family.

These tea sessions created a gentle, predictable space where her grandmother felt valued and heard. The staff reported that her grandmother's mood remained elevated for days afterwards, and she would enthusiastically tell everyone about her granddaughter's next visit.

Those small, intentional moments brought back her grandmother's spark and deepened their connection.

Remember, we can't create meaningful changes without first imagining them. But we don't have to imagine massive transformations – just small, consistent steps forward.

"There are two types of connection: one that is about creating memorable moments that strengthen your bond with deliberate intention, and one that is about practical duties and getting actions completed."

Stop ignoring the gaps

Great connections start with thinking about where the gaps are. You have options for how to assess what your gaps are and imagine the difference between where you are now and where you want to be, even if it's only a 1% improvement. Stop ignoring the gaps. Get clear about what is missing for you and your loved one.

In the next chapter, I will show you how to prepare for these connections by creating the right environment, setting your mindset and using effective strategies to ensure your time together is meaningful and fulfilling. You'll discover practical tips and exercises to make every interaction count, paving the way for deeper relationships and lasting joy.

Chapter three

LIGHTENING YOUR LOAD

A dynamic journey

Life is a dynamic journey characterised by constant change – circumstances, as well as our choices, alter our path. Each decision, no matter how small, opens new doors while closing others.

When we learn that a loved one is facing age-related health challenges or a diagnosis, it transforms our shared journey. This news often arrives like a sudden storm, disrupting our carefully laid plans and expectations.

Common experiences when facing an ageing diagnosis include the following.

Initial impact:
- Processing the diagnosis takes time.
- Facts and figures might blur as emotions take centre stage.
- Time seems both to speed up and slow down.

Shifting dynamics:
- Family roles may reshape themselves naturally.
- Daily routines adapt to new priorities.
- Communication patterns often deepen and change.

Finding balance:
- You learn to navigate between practical needs and emotional support.
- You discover strength in vulnerability.
- You create new ways to connect and share experiences.

Growing together:
- Small moments gain new significance.
- Shared memories become more precious.
- New traditions emerge from changed circumstances.

Your emotional response is uniquely yours. There's no guidebook for processing these changes, only the understanding that every feeling has its place in this journey.

Here are some emotions that may surface for you. After recognising any of these complex emotions in yourself, the next step is transforming how you approach connection with your ageing loved one.

Here are some emotions that may surface for you:

The backpack of life

Think of your life experiences as a backpack. Some days it feels heavy with responsibilities, deadlines and worries. Others it carries treasured memories, wisdom and hope.

The weight in your backpack varies. While memories, wisdom and hope are valuable contents, they too can feel heavy at times – especially memories tinged with regret or complicated emotions. Some burdens weigh more than others.

The key isn't emptying your backpack completely. That's unnecessary – and impossible. Instead, it's about organising its contents more thoughtfully.

When you're carrying a heavy backpack, your instinct is to hurry to get to your destination quickly. However, connecting with ageing loved ones requires us to slow down and be present.

Understanding which contents of your backpack truly matter – which ones are worth carrying – allows you to lighten your load by letting go of what doesn't serve your relationships. This doesn't mean abandoning your responsibilities but rather gaining clarity about what deserves your energy and attention.

Simple ways to lighten your load

Practice the 'three-breath reset' before interactions:

- **Breath 1:** Acknowledge your current emotional state.
- **Breath 2:** Release immediate worries.
- **Breath 3:** Open yourself to connection.

Remember those one percenters we discussed? They work here too. Small adjustments in how you manage your daily load can create significant space for meaningful connection.

Sarah used to arrive at her father's house, mentally reviewing her work deadlines. Now, she uses her drive time to transition, arriving ready to be fully present. "I'm not less busy," she says, "but I'm more intentional about how I carry my responsibilities."

This isn't about achieving perfect balance or becoming stress-free. It's about making conscious choices about what you carry and when you set it down. Think of it as creating breathing space in your backpack of life – just enough room to add fresh memories, shared laughter, and deeper connections with your ageing loved one.

There's a limit to what we can carry

There's a limit to what we can carry in the backpack of life, yet we often ignore this truth. Just as a physical backpack has finite space, our mental and emotional capacity has boundaries. When we exceed these limits, meaningful relationships (especially with ageing loved ones) are usually the first to suffer.

You might think, *I already know what's on my plate. Unpacking my commitment seems unnecessary when I can't do anything about my backpack.* While you may feel familiar with your commitments, our lives often become cluttered without us realising it.

This process isn't about adding another task. It's about gaining clarity and control. Taking a detailed look at your commitments often reveals surprising patterns and time drains that you may never have noticed before.

Consider Sarah again: she's an executive managing a team of 15. Sarah was drowning in responsibilities. Between her leadership role, caring for her ageing father and raising teenage children, she constantly felt scattered.

She shared how she unpacked her metaphorical backpack and discovered she was still handling tasks from a project she'd officially delegated months ago. Her team was capable and had the skills to handle the work, but they lacked the authority to take charge. Once she had handed over these and other legacy tasks, she carved out time for weekly afternoon teas with her father, turning an impossible dream into a cherished routine.

 TAKE ACTION: THE BACKPACK AUDIT

Set aside 30 minutes in a quiet space with a notebook or device.

1. List everything you're currently responsible for.
2. Mark each item as:
   - must carry (essential responsibilities)
   - could share (potential for delegation)
   - need to release (no longer serves your priorities).
3. Estimate the time spent weekly on each item.
4. Highlight items that directly affect the connection with your ageing loved one.

This lays the groundwork for making intentional choices about how you allocate your time and energy, potentially creating more space for meaningful connections with your ageing loved one.

Give what you can (tactically) to someone else to carry

The backpack audit enables you to review the tasks in your life and identify which ones you might delegate to family members, colleagues or professional services. Just as CEOs don't handle operational details, trying to manage all aspects of caring for ageing loved ones isn't just unsustainable – it's counterproductive.

You'll find some things in your backpack you can't throw out, but you can share the load. It's about consciously redistributing it so you can focus on what truly matters, including connecting with your ageing loved one. These won't be easy choices, but they reflect the reality that sometimes our priorities must shift dramatically to accommodate the needs of those we love. Honestly evaluate your current situation. What adjustments – small or substantial – might create the space you need for more meaningful connection?

Effective delegation creates space for what matters

It may create a mix of relief and initial anxiety as you learn to trust others with tasks you've always handled yourself. However, effective delegation of tasks is necessary to create the mental and emotional space needed for meaningful connections with ageing loved ones. When we're bogged down with an endless to-do list, we often find ourselves too drained or distracted to be fully present in our relationships.

As a senior finance manager, Mark used a decision matrix to analyse his weekly commitments. He discovered he was spending three hours each week organising his father's medications, a task his father's carer could handle. This simple delegation created space for Saturday morning garden centre visits with his father, his favourite activity.

You might think, *I can't delegate these tasks. No one else can do them as well as I can, and it's faster if I just do everything myself.* It's natural to feel that way, especially if you've been managing everything on your own for a long time. However, holding onto every task yourself can lead to burnout and limit your ability to focus on what truly matters: connecting with your ageing loved one. While others might not do tasks exactly as you would, the benefit of delegating often outweighs minor differences in execution. Start small. Choose one or two tasks to delegate and gradually increase as you become more comfortable with the process.

Doing everything for someone can be destructive. It puts you in a position of control and self-importance. Sharing the load means being humble and protecting your loved one from being vulnerable. If you don't share the load and you collapse, there's no one else to do what needs to be done.

Make space for self-care

Look at each commitment through two lenses: its impact on family connections and its effect on your energy levels.

David's story shows this perfectly. As a management consultant, he evaluated activities based on both their relationship impact and personal energy cost. His analysis revealed something surprising: his weekly squash game, which triggered guilt, proved essential. That hour of exercise gave him the energy and mental clarity to engage fully with his ageing mother. While on the surface it may appear like an indulgence, given his numerous commitments, it was actually essential for him to keep up the weekly squash game to maintain his other commitments.

You might think, *I barely have enough time to manage my current responsibilities. Won't self-care take away from time with my ageing loved one?*

This common concern misses a crucial point: self-care powers meaningful connection. Think of it like maintaining your car. Skip regular servicing and, eventually, you'll break down – unable to drive anywhere. The same applies to your capacity for care and connection.

You don't need elaborate routines or hours of 'me time'. Start small:

- Take three deep breaths before entering your loved one's home.
- Walk for five minutes during your lunch break.
- Drink your morning tea mindfully, without checking emails.

Making it work

If guilt creeps in when considering self-care, try these approaches:

- Start with micro-actions (two or three minutes daily).
- Integrate care into existing routines.
- Track how your energy affects your interactions.
- Notice improvements in your patience and presence when you take more time for self-care.

"Sometimes you don't get the weight of what you carry until you feel the weight of it releasing."

Remember, your capacity to care depends on your willingness to maintain your own wellbeing. When you nurture yourself, you enhance your ability to nurture others.

A well-organised tool for connection

You've now learned how to transform your backpack from an overwhelming burden into a well-organised tool for connection. Think of it as your personal strategic plan – one that prioritises meaningful relationships while maintaining sustainable energy levels.

Unpacking your commitments creates clarity, revealing what truly matters. Strategic delegation multiplies your impact, while focusing on essential tasks keeps you aligned with your core values. And when you prioritise self-care, you fuel the meaningful connections that matter most.

Now that you've prepared yourself by lightening your load and making space for what matters, it's time to explore how reflection can deepen your connection journey. In the next chapter, we'll discover how balancing head and heart through thoughtful reflection can transform your relationship with your ageing loved one from routine to meaningful. You'll learn practical tools to examine your connection patterns and break free from autopilot mode, creating space for more authentic engagement.

Chapter four

BALANCING YOUR HEAD AND HEART

Moments of reflection

For three years, David visited his mother, Mary, every Wednesday. He drove her to medical appointments and helped with errands. The routine became so automatic that David could practically do it in his sleep. One day, while waiting in yet another doctor's office, David started journalling – something he hadn't done since his mother's dementia diagnosis. As he wrote, he realised he couldn't remember the last genuine conversation he'd had with his mother. Their interactions had become a checklist of medications, appointments, groceries ... repeat.

That evening, instead of rushing through their usual dinner routine, David tried something different. He pulled out an old photo album and simply sat with his mother. To his amazement, his mum became animated, sharing stories about the photos that David had never heard before. That single moment of reflection led David to reshape their weekly visits, creating space for connection alongside care tasks.

Breaking out of autopilot

You are more likely to identify and act on opportunities for meaningful interaction when you reflect. Breaking out of autopilot through regular reflection doesn't just improve the quality of connection, it makes carer tasks more manageable by reducing the emotional drain of disconnected care routines. When we operate on autopilot, we miss subtle cues and opportunities for connection. Regular reflection helps caregivers shift from task-focused to relationship-focused care, which benefits both the caregiver and their loved one.

In this chapter, I will provide you with tools to facilitate regular connection reflection. This chapter examines how stepping back to reflect on our connection patterns can transform relationships from routine to meaningful. Connection reflection is about actively choosing to understand how our experiences with our ageing loved ones feed our narrative, and then how our narrative feeds our experiences. You'll discover simple tools like the head and heart check method and the three-question reflecting practice that will create lasting impact. Most importantly, you'll understand that reflection isn't about dwelling on the past – it's about understanding patterns to create better moments in the future. Quality reflection can give you that break to see the story happening around you and to choose the story you want.

Regular reflection on your connection patterns helps break the autopilot mode many of us fall into when caring for ageing loved ones.

What's the story you are telling yourself?

Conduct a daily or weekly connection reflection – the intentional practice of examining and improving how you interact with your ageing loved one. This involves understanding your thought patterns, emotional responses and behavioural habits that either strengthen or hinder meaningful connections. This is not casual reminiscing or a simple self-review. It is a structured and purposeful examination of your connection patterns, biases and opportunities for growth in relationships with your ageing loved one.

It might feel like taking a step back to observe your interaction patterns, discover emotional barriers you didn't realise existed or find surprising insights about your communication style. But you might uncover something that will help you improve your connection with your ageing loved one, such as: *I never noticed how often I interrupt with solutions. I see now why certain conversations can become tense. I understand what triggers my impatience.* It might seem like a magnifying glass on your relationship dynamics, but it is also a pause button in your carer routine and a reset opportunity for deeper connection.

"Building connection with ageing loved ones is like tending a garden — it requires intention, patience and small, regular acts of care."

TAKE ACTION: HEAD AND HEART

The Head and Heart check method is about using the head to think about what actually happened and the heart to consider how it made you feel.

Here are two practical steps to conduct this check:

1. Keep a simple connection journal. Write down one observation after each interaction.

2. Set a five-minute daily and/or weekly ten-minute reflection appointment with yourself.

Many people find it helpful to give their journal a broader purpose that feels more practical and less like 'homework'. Consider using your journal to track significant events, health matters and meaningful interactions in one place.

This comprehensive approach can serve multiple purposes, helping you monitor important medical information, document changes over time and capture those special moments of connection. This combined approach often feels more sustainable and provides valuable reference information for both care decisions and emotional reflection.

With the head and heart check method, start small and build gradually. Instead of trying to analyse every interaction, choose one brief moment from your day. Use micro-reflections – two-minute check-ins while doing routine tasks like driving home or making coffee.

The goal isn't perfect documentation but rather developing awareness about your connections and what influences them positively or negatively over time.

> **TAKE ACTION: THREE QUICK PROMPTS**
>
> Keep a simple note on your phone with three quick prompts:
>
> 1. What happened?
> 2. How did I feel?
> 3. What's one thing I learned?
>
> This approach bypasses the overwhelm of lengthy reflection. It fits naturally into your day. When emotions feel heavy, focus first on just *observing* rather than *analysing*. Remember, you're building awareness, not solving every challenge at once. The goal is progress, not perfection.

There is a framework in the book *Thinking, Fast and Slow* by Daniel Kahneman that examines how these two things feed each other: we can consider our 'experiential self' and 'narrative self'. Our *experiential self* is the version in our mind that is having the experiences and doing the things, and those experiences drive the narrative that we tell and believe about ourselves. Our *narrative self* drives the experiences that we have – it is circular, and it happens whether we like it or not. With intentional reflection we can actively take control of our narrative self.

The power of journalling

Journalling is a great reflective practice that anyone can get involved in. Hayley Langsdorf from creative consultancy Thoughts Drawn Out reminds us that no one ever has to see your journal: doodle, draw, use words, colours and shapes – it doesn't have to look a particular way. Use it as a place to process the experiences you've had and give them the context of a narrative: start somewhere, understand the experience you go through and talk about where you end up. You can reframe any narrative into a new story that offers a better experience.

Sometimes you must break the cycle, step out and reflect on the story you are perpetuating. Ask yourself, *if I tell this story later, is this the story I want to tell?* If I think about my own scenario with Dad, the narrative I would have told myself is that I was too busy and only had finite time. My rewrite could have been that if I couldn't adjust the time, how could I have acted differently with the time I had?

"Get the brain spaghetti out"

Think about the powerful moments with your ageing loved one. Maybe they're holiday traditions, shared challenges you've overcome or even daily rituals that have become meaningful over time. Reflection doesn't need to be complicated. Find what works naturally for you. Some people prefer quiet contemplation during their morning coffee, others process their thoughts best while walking, and many find clarity through writing.

Getting into a reflective state often works best when we engage multiple senses. The physical act of writing by hand creates a unique connection between our thoughts and actions. When we write, we slow down our racing minds and give shape to our scattered thoughts. As Hayley Langsdorf shares, "Something magical happens when you put pen to paper – you get the brain spaghetti out." This vivid image captures how writing helps untangle our jumbled thoughts and emotions, creating clarity from chaos.

Try different approaches to reflection:

- journal during your morning routine
- voice record your thoughts while driving
- draw or doodle your feelings and memories
- write letters to your loved ones (whether or not you send them)
- create a family memory book together.

You might struggle because maybe there's time pressure and competing priorities or emotional resistance to examining the difficult interactions. Perhaps you have uncertainty about how to reflect effectively or fear of discovering uncomfortable truths. It could be difficult to maintain consistent reflection habits.

Or, you could be feeling vulnerable, examining your own actions and getting stuck in self-criticism rather than growth. You could find it challenging to maintain objectivity, identify patterns in their behaviour and separate facts from emotion.

"Connection doesn't require grand gestures. It can be as simple as sharing a cup of tea and asking one meaningful question."

TAKE ACTION: THREE DEEPER REFLECTION QUESTIONS

Now move on to the three deeper questions. After your next three interactions with your ageing loved one, ask yourself:

1. Which moment felt most authentic?
2. What did I learn about my loved one today?
3. What would I do differently next time?

Make the three deeper questions feel safer and more manageable by treating them like a friendly conversation with yourself rather than a formal analysis. Start by noting just one positive moment from each interaction. This builds confidence and reduces the fear of self-criticism. Write in the third person if it helps you maintain perspective; for example, "Sarah noticed" instead of "I noticed".

Use a simple template with three columns: facts (what actually happened), feelings (your emotional response), and future (one small thing you might try next time). This structure helps separate observations from emotions while keeping the focus on growth rather than judgement. Most importantly, celebrate small insights that often lead to the most meaningful changes.

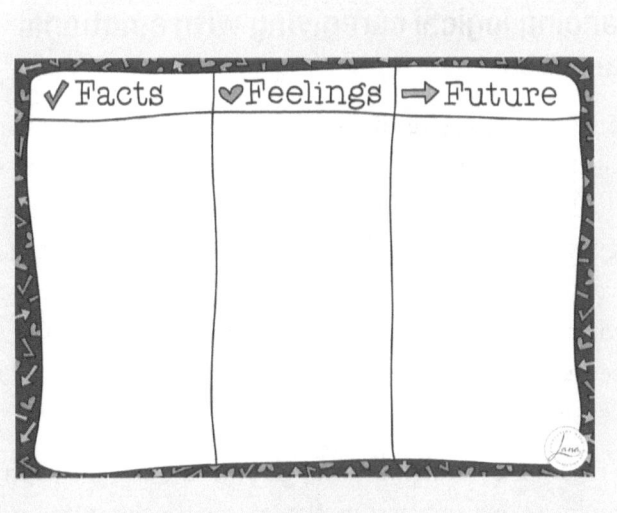

Remember, reflection isn't about perfection – it's about understanding yourself better and deepening your connections with others. Regular reflection helps you notice patterns, appreciate progress and identify opportunities for meaningful interaction with your ageing loved ones.

Balancing logical caregiving with emotional awareness

In this chapter, you've discovered that meaningful connection isn't just about what you do, it's about understanding how you do it. Through reflection, you've learned to balance logical caregiving with emotional awareness, recognise and challenge your assumptions, value multiple perspectives in your caregiving journey, transform daily interactions into opportunities for deeper connection and use self-awareness as a tool for relationship growth.

Stop running on autopilot through your interactions with your ageing loved one and start implementing the pause and process practice. Take time after each visit to reflect on things you've learned about your ageing loved one or yourself. Remember that connecting with your ageing loved one isn't about perfection. It's about being deliberate. The challenges you face as part of the sandwich generation are real, but so is your capacity for creating meaningful moments amid the chaos.

Now that you've developed the practice of reflection to enhance your connections, the next step is to expand your support network. Next, we'll explore building your 'connection ecosystem' – a network that amplifies your ability to nurture relationships with your ageing loved one. Just as businesses thrive through strong partner networks, you'll discover how building a supportive community creates sustainable, enriching connections that benefit everyone involved.

Chapter five

CREATING A CARE SQUAD

An ecosystem of connection

Embrace an ecosystem of connection with others. Think of caring for your ageing loved one like running a family restaurant. Everyone has their role. Some cook – that's you handling the daily tasks. Some wait tables – the siblings who show up occasionally. Someone also needs to manage the books. Hello, paperwork.

No one should be stuck in the kitchen all day. The key is creating your own care squad – a mix of family, friends and helpers who can tap into each other or tap each other in and out. Share the load and pass the tasks around: "Your turn for the doctor's visit, sis. Don't forget to laugh about that time Dad tried to convince the doctor his internet diagnosis was better." When everyone pitches in, even a little, it transforms the situation from overwhelming to manageable. Plus, you get to keep your sanity, which is pretty important too.

Remember, just because you are the star chef, that doesn't mean you have to cook every meal. Sometimes it's okay to let someone else handle the kitchen while you take a much-needed break. When you build this support network, you'll discover you're not alone on this journey. There's something wonderful about sharing both the challenges and the victories with others who get it. Occasionally someone will burn the metaphorical toast, but that adds to the family stories you'll share later.

Making overwhelming situations manageable

When everyone contributes, even in small ways, overwhelming situations become manageable. You maintain your sanity while ensuring quality care for your ageing loved one. This isn't about becoming a lone hero – it's about fostering teamwork and ensuring emotional and physical responsibilities are shared. It might feel like you're stepping into a leadership role, but instead of commanding, you're guiding. Frequent, open conversations where everyone's voice is heard will bring everyone together with a shared purpose, caring for your ageing loved one while supporting each other.

Sarah juggled life in suburban Brisbane, splitting her days between a demanding corporate role, two primary school kids and her mum, who lived alone across town. Sarah was exhausted, guilt-ridden and missing meaningful moments with both her children and her mum. When her friend Katie noticed her struggling and offered to help with school pick-ups, Sarah discovered what research consistently proves – people with strong support networks report less caregiver stress. By creating a network of support, with her brother handling their mum's physio, neighbours sharing meals and colleagues providing workplace flexibility, Sarah found she now had energy for what mattered most: those precious moments connecting with her mum.

Assembling and managing your team

Connection is about everyone who cares for your ageing loved one. Think like a great team leader – they understand everyone's strengths and orchestrate success through teamwork. If you apply this to family care, like any effective leader, you must start by mapping out your team. Who's naturally organised? They're perfect for managing appointments. Who's the social butterfly? They're great for regular check-ins. Who's tech-savvy? They're ideal for setting up video calls. Who's patient? They're wonderful for doctor's visits.

Schedule brief family catch-ups. They don't need to be formal. A WhatsApp group and/or a monthly coffee catch-up can work wonders.

Smart leaders delegate based on skills, not just availability. Your brother might struggle with medical appointments but excel at handling paperwork. Your sister might find shopping stressful but love cooking meals.

Clear communication prevents problems. Keep everyone in the loop with shared calendars or care apps. The best workplace leaders don't create dependency, they build capable teams. That's your goal too – fostering a network of support that makes everyone, including your loved one, feel valued and connected. Like any good leader knows, success isn't about being indispensable; it's about building something sustainable.

Caregiving involves many people. Success is about ensuring that all caregivers feel valued and included in the process, creating a sense of togetherness in providing the best care for your ageing loved one.

Have the conversations before it's too late. What are the decisions that need to be discussed and made together? Who's the right person to step up?

Let's be real. Trying to handle everything yourself isn't just exhausting, it's unsustainable. You know that feeling when you're running on empty, going through the motions and barely keeping your head above water. That's not good for you and definitely not for your loved one.

Small acts add up to something powerful – energy left in your tank to enjoy time with your loved one, share memories and stories, and laugh and be present without watching the clock or mentally ticking off your to-do list. At the end of the day, that's what matters most: quality time, not just task time.

Leading your team

Think of it this way. You're not asking for help because you can't cope. You're creating opportunities for everyone to contribute because it makes the whole experience better for you, them and especially your loved one. Also, someone has to be the leader, so be a good leader and make everyone feel that they matter. Remember how good leaders acknowledge contributions. Thank people. Share positive updates and celebrate the small wins.

Studies by the Family Caregiver Alliance emphasise that shared caregiving responsibilities improve both caregiver wellbeing and the quality of care provided to ageing loved ones. A collaborative caregiving approach reduces stress and provides better outcomes.

You might be thinking, *I'm not a leader. I've never been the leader in our family. I do the work.* Building a connected team reduces your overall workload because you're sharing tasks and emotional support, not taking on more.

A major barrier is the reluctance to ask for help, often out of fear of burdening others. Overcoming this requires realising that sharing the load is beneficial for everyone in the long term. What if no one wants to put up their hand? What about people who are in other cities?

Remember – participation doesn't have to be equal to be fair. Focus on what each person can realistically contribute, even if it's just a weekly phone call or helping with online grocery orders.

Hold brief monthly video calls to check in on how the system is working and adjust as needed. This keeps everyone aligned and ensures no one feels overwhelmed.

 TAKE ACTION: TEAM MEETING

Start by organising a family meeting. Bring together all those involved in your loved one's care and encourage open conversations about responsibilities, concerns and feelings. Begin by asking each person what role they'd like to play. Whether it's small or large, write it down and make sure it's realistic.

Set up a digital hub (like a shared Google Calendar or care coordination app) where family members can see upcoming tasks, mark what they can help with and track what's been done. This makes it easier for everyone to contribute, regardless of their location.

Identify your family's energy barometer

The energy barometer is the family member whose mood and energy levels significantly influence the emotional climate of the whole group. They may not be aware of it, but their emotional state often sets the tone for others. This is not necessarily the most dominant or outspoken person in the family. I am talking about the individual whose attitude, whether positive or negative, subtly impacts the group's overall emotional well-being. It might feel like there's a shift in the room when this person is particularly stressed or calm. People might mirror this individual's tone or mood without even realising it, and it might seem like the family is either more at ease or tenser depending on how this person feels.

We all know that one family member who sets the tone. Maybe it's your mum, who worries constantly about your dad, making everyone else anxious. Maybe it's your sister, who stays positive and somehow gets your dad to take his medicine when no one else can. Notice who this person is in your family. When they're having a good day, everyone has a good day. When they're stressed, everyone feels it.

Supporting this key person isn't complicated – it can be as simple as a quick, "How are you really doing?" check-in, a coffee and chat, taking one task off their plate or keeping them in the loop about good news. These small gestures that help them stay positive create a domino effect of good vibes throughout the family. When the mood-setter is doing okay, everything runs more smoothly.

In a busy household, Jenny noticed how her mum's approach to caring for her dad shifted dramatically based on her older sister Maria's attitude. When Maria got overwhelmed by their

"Creating meaningful connections with ageing loved ones isn't about adding more to your day — it's about making small moments matter."

dad's declining health, her stress rippled through the family. Even their dad became more resistant to care.

After learning about emotional contagion in family dynamics, Jenny started paying attention to Maria's stress signals. She began calling her sister for coffee catch-ups before small problems became big ones. By helping Maria manage her emotions through regular check-ins and shared problem-solving, the whole family dynamic shifted. Dad became more cooperative, the siblings communicated better and care decisions became easier. Most importantly, they rediscovered the joy in family time together.

You might be thinking, *Great, now I need to manage everyone's mood too.* Take a breath. This isn't about adding pressure; it's about noticing what already happens in your family. You probably already know who your family's energy barometer is – the person whose mood shift can turn a smooth care day into chaos or transform a tense situation into a manageable one. Maybe it's you. Maybe it's your brother. Maybe it's even your ageing parent.

Understanding this dynamic isn't about fixing or controlling it. It's about working with it. When you notice your family's energy barometer is struggling, you can step in with support before things escalate, rally others to share the load and adjust plans to reduce pressure. When you work with your family's natural dynamics instead of against them, things flow better. Remember, this isn't another job. It's a tool to help make your existing role easier.

Start the conversation: "Hey, I've noticed our family meetings go so much more smoothly when you're there. You have a way of keeping things on track." Or, "You know what I've realised? When you're feeling good about Dad's care, we all feel more confident. When you're worried, we all get anxious."

Unspoken dynamics create unnecessary stress. Naming them reduces their power.

Here are some practical steps:

- Check in regularly. "Can we grab a coffee? I'd love to hear how you're really doing with all this."
- Create early warning systems. "What tells you that you're getting overwhelmed? How can we spot it early?"
- Develop backup plans. "If you're having a tough day, who would you like us to call first?"
- Create simple support strategies – text updates before big decisions, regular debrief sessions, sharing wins no matter how small, and tag-teaming onerous tasks.
- Use phrases like, "I've got your back on this one. What do you need right now? Let's figure this out together."

It's okay to not be okay sometimes. When you support your family's natural emotional leader, you're making things easier for everyone, including yourself. The struggle may come from the individual not recognising their influence or being resistant to acknowledging their role in the group's emotional dynamic or climate.

Handling disagreements within the team

Disagreements don't have to fuel conflict. Approach conversations with a willingness to learn. You can reframe your story, and then it's easier to listen to what your team is telling you. The quiet ones can have great ideas.

Being humble means approaching decisions with an open mind and a willingness to understand other perspectives, even when they differ from yours. I'm not talking about suppressing your opinions or agreeing with everything others say. This is about respecting others' views, being willing to compromise and finding common ground to move forward.

There might be moments of tension during disagreements, but also relief when conflicts are resolved respectfully. There might be thoughtful pauses in conversation as people take time to consider differing views. It might seem like the family dynamic becomes more understanding.

Sarah's last big project at work was spread across three departments, each convinced that their approach was right. The breakthrough came when the senior manager said, "I might be missing something here. Can you help me understand your perspective?" That simple question changed the path forward.

Sarah applied this at home when coordinating her dad's care. Instead of insisting her schedule was best, she tried, "I'm curious about why evening visits work better for you, Tom?" Her brother explained his kids' morning sports commitments, something she hadn't considered. This shift from "I'm right" to "Help me understand" transformed their family meetings from battlegrounds to brainstorming sessions: "With work, what factors am I not seeing? With your family, what concerns do you have about this care plan?"

Just like in the office, sometimes the best solutions come from asking questions instead of making statements; listening to understand, not to respond; and acknowledging that everyone brings valuable insights. Being humble doesn't mean being a doormat. It means being smart enough to know that no one has all the answers. Real success, whether in business or family care, often starts with five simple words: "What do you think about …?"

Disagreements are inevitable in caregiving. Approaching these conflicts with humility stops everyone descending into the usual Christmas afternoon barney, making it easier to focus on what truly matters – your loved one's care.

During a tense family meeting in their father's living room, Maria sat frustrated as her siblings argued about their dad's new care schedule. As a corporate mediator, she recognised the same patterns she saw in workplace conflicts. Like many families, they were talking at each other, not with each other – leading to increased stress and poor decisions about their dad's care.

Drawing from studies in workplace conflict resolution, Maria introduced a simple rule: before disagreeing, each person had to accurately summarise the other person's point of view.

The change was huge. Their meetings became more productive, decisions more unified and, most importantly, their dad noticed, commenting that things felt easier between them all. The research was right. The same skills that build strong business teams can transform family caregiving from a battlefield to a partnership.

You might think this means giving up too much control. Being humble doesn't mean losing control. It means building stronger, more collaborative relationships where everyone's voice is valued.

Sometimes conflict can't be resolved with the best will in the world, even though you are listening and being humble. You have to find other ways to solve the conflict, because you need the ecosystem to create meaningful moments. Try mediation, counselling, lawyers, self-help groups and friends.

Being nice often isn't enough. You've tried the coffee chats, you've listened patiently, you've bent over backwards to accommodate everyone; but sometimes, despite your best efforts, you're still stuck. That's okay. It's normal. There are options.

Start small. Join an online caregiver support group. Talk to a trusted friend who's been through this. Connect with your GP for local resources.

Get professional help early and don't wait for a crisis. Consider family counselling. Many offer telehealth options. A geriatric care manager for neutral guidance or a mediator experienced in elder care can be a lifesaver for your sanity.

Create a backup system. Build connections outside your immediate family. Develop relationships with neighbours. Connect with local community services. Remember, getting help isn't admitting defeat. It's being smart enough to know that some situations need fresh eyes.

Write down what's not working before seeking help. It makes that first conversation with a professional much more productive.

Your energy is better spent creating memorable moments with your loved one than arguing about who should do what. Sometimes, the strongest thing you can say is, "I think we need some help with this." Your loved one deserves a united care team, even if you need some outside support to create it.

Stop trying to handle everything alone

In this chapter, you've learned that creating an ecosystem of connection is key to reducing stress and fostering deeper relationships in the caregiving process. It's about sharing the load, recognising emotional influences and approaching differences with humility. By leading with openness, understanding emotional dynamics and embracing collaboration, you're building a supportive environment where you, your team and your loved one can thrive.

It's completely okay – even necessary – to simply ask others for help. This straightforward act can be surprisingly empowering. If you're surrounded by good people, you'll often find they're more than willing to lend a hand. Many people want to help but don't know how unless you specifically ask. Your request gives them the opportunity to contribute in meaningful ways.

Now you know how to create a connected ecosystem where everyone plays a role in caring for your ageing loved one. You've embraced collaboration, recognised emotional dynamics and approached differences with humility.

In the next chapter, I will show you how to take these connections to the next level with a connection challenge. This challenge will offer you exciting choices to deepen your bonds, strengthen your caregiving team and create moments of joy and meaning with your loved one. Get ready to test your connection skills and see how small, intentional actions can make a big difference.

Chapter six

YOUR CONNECTION CHOICES

Discovering a new rhythm

There are many ways to make a deeper connection with your ageing loved one. You have choices, and they don't have to take much time. Connection choices mean intentionally choosing ways to bond with ageing loved ones, based on your available time and taking part in structured activities that build lasting relationships.

Many people worry that I'm suggesting they have to carve even more time out of their already jam-packed schedules. But it's not about that. It's about not wasting the time that you have with your ageing loved one. Not everything has to be a long phone call. Later in the chapter, I'll give some inspiring examples of how clients I've worked with have turned small moments into something special. I'm also going to give you a list of ways to do the same with your own ageing loved one. It might feel like discovering a new rhythm in your relationship where even small moments carry significance. It could be finally having a framework to turn everyday interactions into opportunities for deeper connection.

A connection choices framework transforms the overwhelming task of staying connected into manageable, actionable choices that fit real life. It empowers you to move from guilt about not doing enough to confidence in making the most of whatever time you have.

You don't need more time

It was a typical Tuesday evening. Mara, a busy marketing executive and mother of two, sat at her desk, staring at her phone. Her father's number had popped up three times that day, but between client meetings and school pickups, she hadn't found the right time to call back. For months, their conversations had become increasingly superficial – quick chats about doctors' appointments and medications.

Mara felt the growing distance between them, remembering how they used to share long conversations about books and politics. The guilt of not making enough time for meaningful connection weighed heavily on her, but the demands of her sandwich-generation life seemed overwhelming. Mara was a client, and we had talked about this in several of our sessions – I'd shared the idea of micro moments of connection – instead of waiting for perfect timing, creating small, intentional interactions could build stronger bonds.

Shortly afterwards, when feeling guilty about her dad, Mara remembered our conversation. She realised she'd been overlooking opportunities throughout her day – her morning coffee time, her lunch break, even her commute – to make that time for her dad. She started small the next morning. Instead of scrolling through emails during her coffee break, she called her dad.

Rather than jumping straight into tasks and schedules, she asked him about the book she'd noticed on his shelf during her last visit. This simple shift in approach put their relationship on a fresh path. Their daily 50-minute chats became a fun ritual. Her father started saving interesting newspaper articles to discuss with her, and she found herself jotting down questions she wanted to ask him during the next call. Three months later, during a family dinner, Mara's daughter asked why Grandpa seemed different lately. He was telling more stories and laughing more. Mara smiled, knowing that those small intentional moments had gradually rebuilt the bridge between them.

Mara hadn't found more time. Instead, she discovered that authentic connection doesn't require grand gestures or perfect circumstances. It grows through consistent, purposeful choices to be present in whatever time you have. Small changes in how we approach connection could profoundly impact our relationships with our ageing loved ones. It's not about finding more time – it's about making different choices with the time we have.

Making time for more meaningful connections with your ageing loved one also doesn't require a complete life overhaul. This chapter shows you how to create significant moments of connection that naturally fit into your schedule, whether you have 30 minutes or several hours to spare. You'll discover practical strategies for turning everyday interactions into opportunities for deeper connection, applying the SMILE framework that we explored in chapter two. We'll look at specific activities and approaches that match different time windows, helping you move from *I should connect more* to *I know how to make this count*. Then I'll introduce the seven-day connection challenge and a month of connection choices – structured approaches that help you build consistent connection habits. These frameworks provide the gentle support and motivation needed to transform good intentions into meaningful actions.

"The greatest gift you can give your ageing loved one isn't found in a store — it's found in the moments you choose to be present."

The goal isn't to add obligations to your list, but rather to provide clear pathways that make connection more natural and fulfilling for both you and your ageing loved one. By the end of this chapter, you'll have clear, actionable ways to strengthen your relationship with your ageing loved one, regardless of your schedule's demands.

Quick and deep connections

I'm not talking about forcing lengthy visits or complex activities. I am talking about matching connection opportunities to your available time windows, whether it's a 15-minute call or a full day together. You'll feel more like saying a confident "Yes, I can do that", when opportunities arise. It might seem like finally having permission to make the most of small time windows rather than waiting for perfect moments.

Many people feel guilty about 'only' having brief moments to connect, believing that short interactions somehow mean they care less. This guilt can prevent us from reaching out at all – we think, *if I can't spend a proper amount of time, why bother?*

But here's the truth: your ageing loved one values consistency over duration. A regular 10-minute chat where you're fully present means more than an occasional long visit where you're distracted or stressed. These small touchpoints build trust and maintain connection, creating a pattern your loved one can look forward to.

Think of connection like watering a plant – frequent small amounts keep it thriving better than occasional flooding. Your ageing loved one doesn't measure your love by minutes spent together but by the quality of attention you bring to whatever time you have.

This means you act now rather than waiting for ideal circumstances, reducing the risk of future regret.

> **TAKE ACTION: ANALYSE YOUR DAY**
>
> List your typical daily time blocks – 15 minutes, 30 minutes, one hour. Match connection activities to each time block. Schedule regular check-ins using your most common time block and apply the SMILE framework, even in brief interactions.
>
> You might struggle to do this because you have difficulty breaking old patterns and a fear of seeming rushed or having competing priorities. Share your time constraints openly with your ageing loved one. They may appreciate the honesty. For example, "I have 20 minutes before I pick up the kids and I'd love to hear about your day." Set specific triggers for connection, such as driving home after work.

My sister does this with our mum – each evening as she drives home from work, she calls Mum for a chat. This 15-minute window has become time for both of them. What makes this routine so effective is its predictability. My sister catches Mum before dinner, and Mum looks forward to these calls. For my sister, it's a great transition between work and home life – a peaceful interlude before she steps into the evening rush.

The beauty lies in the simplicity. The calls don't need to be long or cover significant topics. Sometimes they discuss a TV show they both watch; other times they just share updates about their respective days. The consistency matters more than the content.

The connection challenge

A seven-day connection challenge and a month of choices will re-establish connection with your ageing loved one and create a habit that helps you keep the connection going. It's something I've done in the workplace on a variety of different topics, including a successful series focused on wellbeing.

This connection challenge is a structured program that guides you through daily connection activities, followed by a month of intentional connection decisions. It's not a rigid schedule of tasks. It's a flexible framework that helps build connection habits through achievable daily actions. It may feel like having a supportive guide through the process of strengthening relationships. It might provide daily wins and small victories, or, finally, a clear path to follow. Structure and accountability help turn good intentions into consistent action, leading to lasting change in relationships. They also deliver an opportunity to choose new options you may not have considered.

Jenny stood in her kitchen one Sunday evening, staring at her mother's missed call from three days ago. As a nurse and mother of teenagers, her days were a blur of shifts, sports practices and household management. The last proper conversation with her mum had been … she couldn't even remember. The final straw came when her daughter mentioned Grandma seemed sad lately, saying she missed their old Sunday dinners. Jenny realised she'd fallen into a pattern of "I'll call tomorrow" that turned into weeks of silence. The thought of rebuilding their connection felt overwhelming. Where would she even start?

I knew Jenny from work and had talked with her about this idea. She took the seven-day connection challenge, followed by deliberate choices over the next month. Instead of trying to reinvent their relationship overnight, it was about small daily actions.

Day one was simple: send a photo of something that made her think of her loved one. Jenny sent her mum a picture of the recipe book they had prepared together when she first moved out. Her mum replied within minutes, sharing a story about teaching Jenny to make scones. That small exchange led to a video call while Jenny made those scones. Through the challenge and into the month of choices, Jenny and her mum found their rhythm. They started with photos and a quick voice message. Then they moved to cooking together over video calls on a Sunday. The teenagers joined in learning family recipes and hearing stories about their mum's childhood.

Six weeks later, Jenny's colleague remarked on how she seemed more grounded despite their hectic schedule. Jenny realised that what had started as a challenge had become a natural part of her routine. She wasn't finding more time; she was using it differently. Those small, consistent connections had rebuilt the bridge between them, one day at a time. It wasn't just that new habits formed. Structured challenges provided the framework needed to turn good intentions into lasting change. Through small, consistent actions, Jenny discovered that meaningful connection could fit into even the busiest life.

You might think, *I can't commit to a daily challenge with my schedule*. The challenge is designed to be flexible, with options for different time commitments. Success isn't about perfection, it's about progress.

> **TAKE ACTION: THE SEVEN-DAY CONNECTION CHALLENGE**
>
> Complete the seven-day connection challenge and use the connection choice calendar – both can be found on the *Connection with Lana* website: connectionwithlana.com. Choose your preferred time block for each day. Select one connection activity from the provided options. Track your experience in the response and adjust your choices based on what works best.

7 DAYS OF CONNECTION CHALLENGE

DAY 1

Share memories together: Take a walk down memory lane with your loved one. Ask them to share their favourite memory with you. You can even ask them to show you old photos or memorabilia from their past.

DAY 2

Cook a meal together: Cooking a meal together is a great way to bond and learn something new. Ask your loved one to share a favourite recipe with you and work together to prepare it.

DAY 3

Play a game together: Playing games is a fun way to connect with your loved one. You can play a board game, a card game or even a video game. Ask your loved one if they have a favourite game they would like to play.

DAY 4

Go for a walk together: Going for a walk is a great way to get some fresh air and exercise while bonding with your loved one. You can explore a new area or walk around your neighbourhood.

DAY 5

Watch a movie together: Watching a movie is a relaxing way to spend time with your loved one. Ask them if they have a favourite movie they would like to watch together.

DAY 6

Listen to music together: Listening to music can be a powerful way to connect with your loved one. Ask them to share their favourite songs with you and take turns listening to each other's favourite music.

DAY 7

Write letters to each other: Writing letters is a thoughtful way to communicate with your loved one. Take the time to write a heartfelt letter to each other, sharing your thoughts and feelings. You can even exchange your letters at the end of the day.

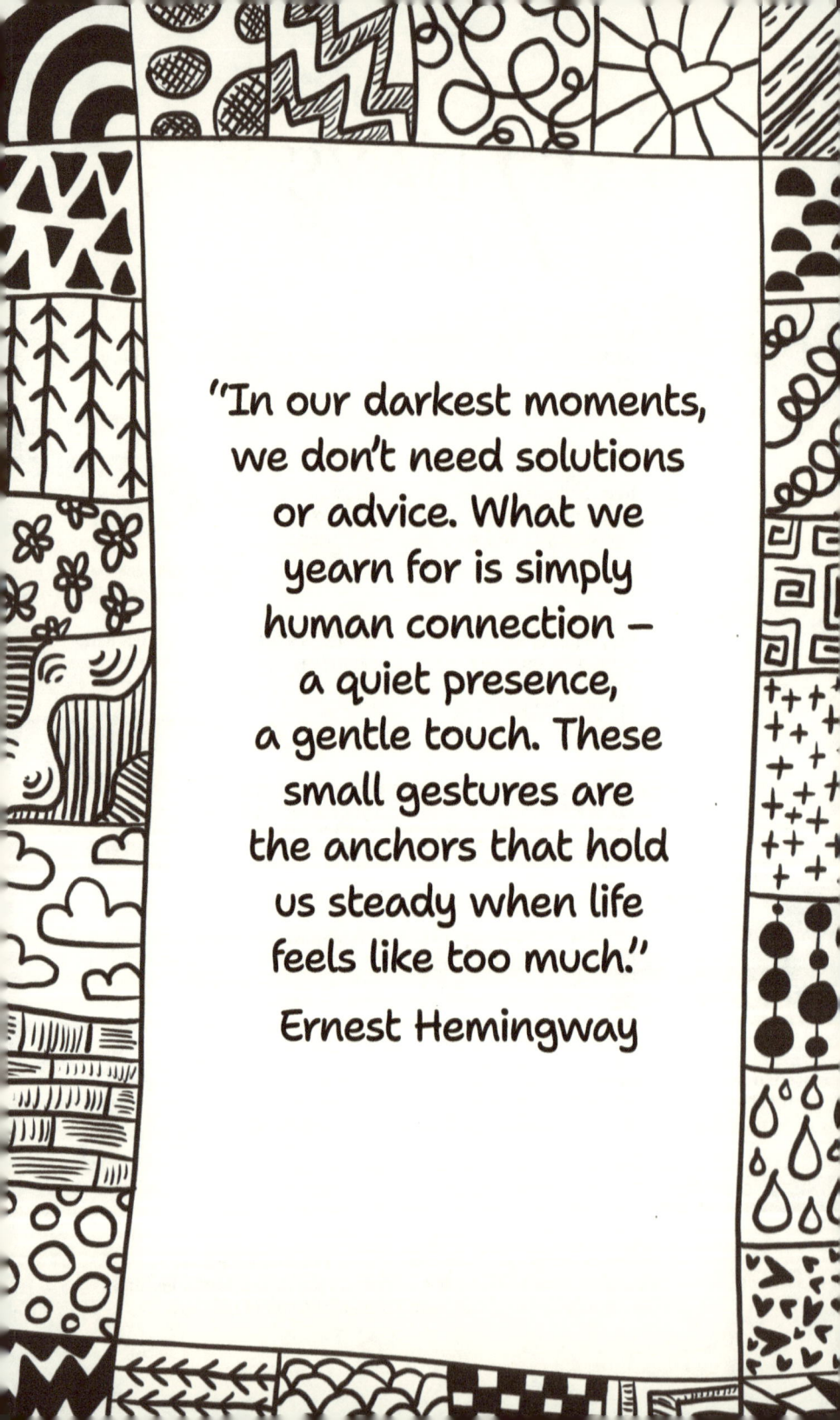

"In our darkest moments, we don't need solutions or advice. What we yearn for is simply human connection — a quiet presence, a gentle touch. These small gestures are the anchors that hold us steady when life feels like too much."

Ernest Hemingway

You might struggle to maintain momentum, handle setbacks, balance competing priorities or overcome resistance from loved ones. Share your journey with a friend who can check in weekly. Set up a 'connection success Sunday' to reflect on what worked and plan the week ahead. Follow the two-day rule, where you never miss more than two days of connection in a row. Use connection stacking, based on the concept of habit stacking from James Clear's book *Atomic Habits*. Combine connection with existing activities. For example, call while walking the dog.

Stop waiting for the perfect time

You've learned how to match connection activities to available time. Start fitting connections into the time you have now. Now you know how to make connection choices that fit your life and build consistent habits through structured approaches like the seven-day connection challenge.

The time you invest in connection now becomes the memories you'll treasure later – whether you have five minutes or five hours to spare.

Most importantly, you understand this journey isn't about adding more to your already full plate – it's about bringing intention to what you're already doing.

Every small choice to connect mindfully creates positive change in your relationship with your ageing loved one.

In the next chapter, I'll show you how to apply your skills to intergenerational connection, creating bridges between different age groups that enrich everyone involved.

Chapter seven

CREATING INTERGENERATIONAL CONNECTIONS

The fabric that holds families together

When your children and your parents connect meaningfully, everyone grows stronger. The simple moments you create today become the foundation of your family's story and legacy.

Intergenerational connection is an exchange where each person shares their perspective and the others take the time to consider, acknowledge and value it. I'm not suggesting you force your kids to see their grandparents or chat on the phone or Skype for lengthy periods – these are surface-level interactions that maintain appearances. This is about creating genuine bonds between generations through intentional, meaningful engagement that enriches everyone. Stories are shared, wisdom flows both ways, and each person feels truly seen and valued.

You may suggest to your mum that she share a particular story you know your kids will enjoy. I do this now with both of my kids. It can be fun, for example, to have all three generations in the kitchen baking an old family recipe. This isn't my thing, but I know others who love it. The experience creates those natural moments where age differences fade away, replaced by genuine curiosity and connection. When done right, everyone walks away feeling energised rather than drained, and looking forward to the next interaction rather than dreading it. It's also about creating the fabric that holds families together, strengthens their ties and brings them closer.

When generations disconnect, we lose more than family ties. We lose irreplaceable knowledge, stories and opportunities for growth.

In this chapter, you'll discover practical ways to strengthen the bonds between different generations of your family. I'll share proven approaches that work in real life, even when time is limited and family dynamics are complicated. We'll explore why casual interactions aren't enough, learn simple conversation starters that spark meaningful discussions, and turn everyday moments into opportunities for deeper connection. You'll find authentic examples from families who've successfully built stronger connections, quick-start actions you can try today, and practical solutions to common challenges. Each section gives you tools to create meaningful connections between generations without adding stress to your already full schedule. Building intergenerational connections isn't about perfection. It's about taking small, intentional steps that add up to lasting family bonds.

An opportunity for growth

Many of us worry our kids will find looking after their grandparents off-putting and that they shouldn't see the difficulties their grandparents are facing. Teenagers often have their own problems, and it seems like they might find their grandparents' issues too much. We also see it as our responsibility to deal with.

When you invite your kids to be part of it, they learn how to have conversations with people beyond their peer group. They develop their empathy muscle and see how tough old age can be. They learn stuff about older generations they didn't know, and they get to tap into the wisdom that comes from age and experience. There are so many rewards. When your kids become involved, some tricky topics will come up: death, illness, the medical system, fairness, and finding solutions to icky situations. You may find this challenging, which might be why you are keeping the kids at bay.

If you get the younger generation more involved, you and your mum or dad will appreciate your teenager's energy, tech-savvy, and willingness to laugh. Your teenager and parents will appreciate your kindness and practicality. Your kids and you appreciate your parents' wisdom and insights.

The reality is that teenagers can be selfish and self-absorbed, so you need to keep your expectations real. If they remember the key dates – the birthdays, the anniversaries and the commemorations – that's cool. Sure, they might have stopped sleeping over, but you can help evolve the relationship as each gets older. My daughter still arranges sleepovers with her Nan every holiday. My son doesn't, but he occasionally pops in for dinner or a chat before his footy training.

Applying your mindset to multiple generations means consciously creating opportunities where everyone involved in caring for your ageing loved one can contribute and benefit, each bringing their unique perspective and receiving value from the interaction.

It might involve your teenage son teaching his grandfather to use a new app while his grandfather shares stories about his own teenage years, both walking away with new insights. Maybe your mother's carer shares observations that help you understand subtle changes in her needs, while you share family traditions that help the carer provide more personalised support. It might look like a family meeting where everyone from your young niece to your elderly aunt contributes ideas about making family gatherings more inclusive and enjoyable for your ageing parent. When done well, these connections create a supportive network.

When you encourage your kids to spend more time with their grandparents, you're not just solving today's challenges for both sides, you're building valuable life skills on both sides and emotional intelligence that benefits everyone. Meanwhile, ageing loved ones who feel they're contributing to the younger generation's growth often show improved mental health and a stronger sense of purpose. The key isn't just about managing care. It's about turning care into an opportunity for everyone to grow together.

Linda was struggling to balance caring for her mother while raising three teenagers, and she decided to change her approach.

Instead of keeping care tasks to herself, she created connection Sundays, where her teens took turns at teaching their grandmother new technology or helping prepare her favourite meals. The results surprised everyone. Her mother's social engagement improved significantly. Her teenagers developed practical skills and emotional maturity. Most importantly, Linda's own stress levels dropped. What she thought would be extra work actually made everything easier. As she explained, "The kids started noticing things I'd missed, and their fresh perspective often led to better solutions."

When we stop seeing elder care as a burden to protect children from and start seeing it as an opportunity for growth, the entire family dynamic shifts positively.

You might think, *this all sounds good in theory, but my family is different. My teenagers are already overwhelmed with school and activities. My ageing parents are resistant to change, and I can barely manage the basics of care. Adding more people to the mix will create stress and complications.* I get it. Many families start from exactly this position.

Throughout this book, I've recommended small steps at every challenge. In this case, these are natural connection points that already exist in your day. For example, instead of creating new activities or responsibilities, look at what's already happening. If your teenager is helping set up a phone, that's a perfect opportunity for them to spend 10 minutes showing their grandparent one useful feature. You don't need to revolutionise your entire care approach overnight. Even one small positive interaction a week can start shifting the dynamic for everyone.

"Don't think about walking in someone's shoes — learn to listen to the story they tell about what it's like in their shoes, and believe them even when it doesn't match your own experience."

TAKE ACTION: THREE-GENERATION SHARE

Create a three-generation share at your next family meal or visit. Ask each person, youngest to oldest, to share one thing they'd like to learn from another generation. For example, your child might want to learn about what games grandma played as a kid. You might want to learn a social media tip from your teenager. Your parent might want to learn how to video-call friends. Set a timer for five minutes per teaching moment. Let each person be both teacher and student.

This simple activity helps everyone feel valued for their knowledge. They can learn something new, connect through shared experiences and see each other in a different light. The beauty of this is that it fits into something you're already doing. Having a meal or a visit takes only 45 minutes or maybe longer, but it creates natural opportunities for future conversations.

Keep track of what each person wants to learn. On busy days when you feel disconnected, you can quickly spark engagements by referring to these interests.

The first time you do this, you might feel self-conscious. Some days you'll get just one person sharing something small. That's perfectly fine. Success isn't measured by how closely you follow the format but by those moments of genuine connection, however brief.

Transform challenges into deeper understanding

Building lasting family legacies and transforming challenges means consciously capturing and sharing the stories, wisdom and values that shape your family while using current difficulties as stepping stones for deeper understanding. It's about finding meaning in the journey of caring for your ageing loved one that extends beyond the present moment. This is not about simply recording family history or creating a photo album. It's about living memories.

It might involve being moved by your mum's stories about immigrating to country Australia from overseas. It might sound like your children asking why celebrating St Patrick's Day is so important, or helping their grandparent with getting Zoom set up on their phone. It might look like transforming a doctor's explanation about your mum's cancer into a chance for your teenager to learn about empathy and other skills they'll carry forward in life.

When done thoughtfully, this approach helps family members find purpose in difficult moments. It creates natural opportunities for sharing wisdom. It also builds resilience through shared challenges, leaving everyone with something meaningful to carry forward. The experience becomes less about plotting out a cancer treatment and more about talking about death, loss, grief and the medical system.

Many families focus solely on getting through the difficult moments of caring for an ageing loved one, seeing each challenge as something to overcome and forget. How we handle these moments shapes our children's future approach to adversity and family bonds. We are teaching the next generation how

"Every shared story, every gentle touch, every moment of laughter builds a bridge between generations that time cannot break."

to face life's difficulties with grace, wisdom and connection. They don't just learn about elder care. They develop crucial life skills, problem-solving, emotional intelligence and the ability to find meaning in difficult situations. These skills become part of your own family's legacy, passed down and strengthened through generations.

The Reeds were struggling with their 75-year-old mother Anna's increasing forgetfulness. Instead of hiding the challenges, they started a simple family tradition called Story Sundays. During weekly video calls, when Anna would repeat stories, rather than showing frustration, Bell would ask her daughter Emma to record these stories in a digital journal. What began as a way to manage repetitive conversations transformed their family dynamic. Emma noted at first, "I thought Grandma repeating stories was annoying. Then I started to notice different details each time. I learned about her childhood in ways I wouldn't have otherwise." The activity not only preserved family history but also helped Emma develop patience and empathy.

Most importantly, the family reported their stress levels dropped: "It's not about avoiding the hard parts; it's about finding purpose in them. Now these stories are part of our family legacy, and my daughter has learned skills she'll carry forward in her own life."

Creating a legacy

Legacy creation might sound a bit depressing. When you're in the thick of caregiving, it can also feel like adding pressure. Remember, some of the most valuable family legacies come from seeing how we handle real, messy, imperfect situations with grace and honesty.

It's not about creating perfect moments or documenting everything. It's about being able to look back at how you showed up and behaved for your ageing loved one at their end stage of life.

The true legacy emerges from your consistent presence, your willingness to navigate difficult conversations and your commitment to connection even when it's challenging. It's found in the small kindnesses, the patient responses when your ageing loved one tells the same story for the third time, and the dignity you help preserve when circumstances are difficult.

Years from now, what will matter most isn't whether you created elaborate memory books or recorded their life story (though these can be wonderful if they feel right for your situation). What will matter is that you were there – truly *there* – listening, caring and connecting in whatever ways were possible given your unique circumstances.

This authentic connection becomes the legacy you carry forward and the example you set for others who may one day care for you.

TAKE ACTION: SUNDAY SNIPPETS

Start a Sunday snippets tradition, a five-minute weekly family check-in focused on one simple question: what did someone in the family teach you this week?

Maybe you're thinking, *everyone in my family is scattered across different time zones, and getting my teenage children to participate in family activities is like pulling teeth. Plus, some weeks are so challenging, finding anything positive feels impossible.*

When families are scattered, memories are fragile and teenagers are reluctant, the Sunday snippets tradition can still work – just differently. Transform it into a flexible family sharing space. Use a group chat where everyone can drop in brief moments of connection wherever they happen. Someone might share a quick photo of grandma's smile, a voice message about a morning breakthrough or a simple text about something that worked well today. There's no pressure for deep insights or regular participation, just an open invitation to notice and share small moments of learning and connection. Over time, these casual contributions build to a meaningful connection of family memories and wisdom captured in a way that works for your real-life situation.

"When it comes to connection with our ageing loved ones, our shared story and shared narrative is an emotive and connective place."

Hayley Langsdorf

Intergenerational connection benefits everybody

In this chapter, you've discovered that intergenerational connection makes both sides happier, and you will feel happier too. You've set your expectations realistically but can still get your kids involved. The road ahead might still have its challenges, but you're now quick to turn these into opportunities for growth and connection. Your job isn't to create more moments, but to notice and nurture the ones that naturally occur.

Think of what you've learned as a toolkit for connection – practical approaches you can adapt to your family's unique situation.

You might be thinking, *I'll start those family conversations once things settle down,* or, *we'll record Mum's stories when she's having a better day,* or, *I'll involve the kids more when everyone's less busy.* But there will never be a perfect moment. While you're waiting for the ideal time, precious opportunities slip away.

Start noticing opportunities in your existing routine – that five-minute drive to a doctor's appointment is a chance to ask one question about their childhood or share a quick memory.

In the next chapter, I'll show you how to master these connections through techniques and strategies that deepen your relationships even further. You'll discover practical ways to track your connection progress, notice patterns that strengthen your family bonds and celebrate small wins you might be missing.

Chapter eight

MASTERING CONNECTION

Creating deeper bonds

You can master connection through the deepening of bonds with your ageing loved one. You've learned the foundations of connecting with your ageing loved one, and now it's time to take those skills further.

This chapter focuses on creating deeper, more meaningful connections while managing the practical demands of care. Connection mastery means developing the internal awareness, flexibility and emotional intelligence needed to create deeper connections with ageing loved ones. This includes releasing preconceptions, embracing vulnerability and approaching connection with curiosity. This involves not simply following a prescribed set of rules but shifting how you show up in relationships with your ageing loved ones. It's about being present, authentic and open to growth.

It might feel like catching yourself before reacting to your mum criticising your new jacket and choosing to respond, "Oh, don't you like this colour on me?" It's finding humour in those challenging situations and being comfortable saying, "I don't know, but let's figure it out together." You might say things like, "What makes you think that way? I'm struggling with this too. I appreciate your perspective." Maybe you're more patient with yourself and others, finding joy in the simple moments and building trust through consistency.

For some, connection is a huge motivator. You want to get better at it, and the better you get, the more you want. This chapter is about how to achieve that. This is about how to go further, and it's mainly for you because you're that kind of person. (I know that because you are reading this book.)[4]

The difference between merely caring for an ageing loved one and truly connecting with them is like the difference between keeping a plant alive and helping it thrive. Mastering connection transforms routine tasks into meaningful moments, reducing your future regret and creating lasting memories. You'll enjoy the connection more. By mastering connection now, you give yourself and your ageing loved one the profound gift of being truly seen, heard and valued in your remaining time together.

Missed opportunites

Not long ago, I sat with Michelle at her kitchen table. She sat with her coffee mug and tears were rolling down her face.

---

[4] This mastery is super helpful at work too. It creates the kinds of bonds that transform everyday workplace interactions into meaningful relationships built on trust and understanding. The same principles that strengthen family bonds – active listening, emotional awareness and genuine curiosity – are powerful tools for professional growth and organisational effectiveness.

"It's been five years since Dad died," she said, "and you know what keeps me awake at night? Not the big moments we missed, but the small things I never asked him about." Michelle was a dedicated daughter. She drove her father to every medical appointment, managed his medications, kept his house clean and coordinated his care. "I did everything right," she whispered. "I was there every single day, but I was so focused on doing things for him, I forgot to just be with him."

She reached for an old photo on her counter – her father, young and strong, standing next to a vintage car. "I found this while clearing out his garage. I have no idea what this car meant to him. Was it his first? Did he restore it? Did he take Mum on dates in it? All these little stories are gone, and the worst part is I had hundreds of opportunities to ask. All those drives to appointments, all those afternoons of sorting pills, I could have asked anything, but instead we talked about his medications."

But Michelle's story does have a second chapter. When her mother started showing signs of memory loss, Michelle did not let moments slip by. She started turning routine tasks into opportunities for connection. Now, organising her mum's weekly pill box becomes a time for sharing stories. Each pill is a pause for a question. "Mum, what was your first job? Tell me about your favourite birthday. What did you dream of becoming when you were young?" Those 15 minutes of sorting medications have become their most precious time together.

One time while Michelle was sorting her vitamins, her mum told her about her first kiss. She was laughing so hard, she could barely finish the story. Michelle told me, "I never knew my quiet mother was quite the rebel in her youth. That's the difference between now and then. I'm still doing all the same tasks for Mum that I did for Dad, but now every moment has the potential for connection. Every task is an opportunity and not just a checkbox."

She picked up the photo of her father again. "I can't go back and ask Dad about this car, but I can make sure that when my kids look at photos of their grandmother years from now, they'll know the stories, because I learned to master connection before it was too late."

In this chapter, we'll explore practical ways to experiment with different approaches while staying authentic. You'll learn why humour matters, how to handle challenging moments and what to do when things don't go as planned. Most importantly, you'll gain confidence in creating connections that feel natural and meaningful for both you and your loved one. Mastering connection isn't about being perfect; it's about being present and intentional in the moments you have together.

Previous chapters focused on understanding connection and building basic skills. This chapter helps you take your relationship deeper. Think of it like learning to dance. First you learn the basic steps, then it's time to find your natural rhythm and style. You'll discover how to shift your mindset from task-focused to relationship-focused, turning routine moments into opportunities for meaningful connection.

The connection mindset shift

Let's establish the mindset that will support your journey to a deeper connection. You should now have a base of confidence in practising the approaches in chapter five, and you have decided you're ready to live in the moment and allow the connection to be more intuitive or fluid. You now must prepare for that.

"The beauty of connecting with ageing loved ones lies not in the length of time spent but in the quality of attention given."

Start by simply deciding to begin. Take opportunities as they come – even if it means missing an appointment or two. True connection often happens outside the plan.

Creating your connection mindset means developing an internal compass that guides how you think, feel and act during interactions with your ageing loved one. This mindset combines self-awareness, emotional intelligence and intentional presence. Gentle curiosity replaces problem-solving. Your words flow from genuine interest rather than obligation. Your conversations shift from tactical updates to meaningful exchanges, creating space for both everyday chat and deeper sharing. This is not about memorising communication techniques or forcing yourself to be something you are not. This is about crafting a natural, authentic way of being that makes meaningful connection more instinctive.

It might feel like releasing the constant pressure to fix everything. You'll discover a natural rhythm between doing and being, like finding your balance on a bicycle. The more relaxed you become, the smoother the ride gets. Each interaction becomes less about ticking boxes and more about tuning into the present moment.

Getting into the right mindset for connection mastery will set you up to cruise through your relapses into busyness and impatience and stay focused on the longer-term goal. You might be thinking, *I don't have the mental bandwidth to change my mindset or think deeply about connection. My loved one needs practical help more than they need meaningful conversations.* But your mindset shift will make practical tasks easier and more efficient, not harder. For example, a medication routine that used to be stressful becomes a natural time for sharing stories, making the task more enjoyable for both of you.

You're not choosing between practical care and connection; you're combining them to create better outcomes for everyone.

 TAKE ACTION: FIND CLARITY

Grab a pen or a device, and become clear about what you want from shifting your mindset. Evolve to a more masterful form of connection. You might struggle with this because when you sit down to write, your mind goes blank or you overthink it. Keep it simple. Start with three bullet points:

- Today I noticed ...
- Next time I might ...
- I felt most connected when ...

For example, "Today I noticed how Mum's eyes lit up when I asked about her favourite song at choir. She started humming it and shared a story about when she first heard it. Next time I might play some of her favourite songs when we're in the car. Music sparks joy and memories for both of us, making car trips a bit of fun. I felt most connected when we both started singing together."

"Time with ageing loved ones is like water in our hands — we can't hold onto it forever, but we can choose how we use each drop."

From small talk to deep connection

Understanding different conversation levels helps us recognise where we typically connect with our ageing loved ones and where we might want to go deeper. Heidi Priebe is a psychologist who talks through a framework outlining three levels of conversation that build upon each other, creating a deeper connection with each layer. The three levels are informational, personal and relational.

I'm going to broaden these out to five levels and use examples with our ageing loved ones:

Level 1 is basic pleasantries, which is where many of us get stuck with our ageing loved ones, especially when we focus on tasks.

Level 2 involves the exchange of facts, such as discussing doctor's appointments. While necessary, staying at this level can leave us feeling disconnected.

Level 3 is where we begin to share opinions and preferences, and could include family decisions, current events or changes in the care circle. This level creates more engagement as we learn about each other's perspectives and values.

Level 4 is where the real connection forms. We share our emotions, fears, hopes and vulnerabilities. With our ageing loved ones, this might mean discussing their feelings about losing independence, or our own feelings about seeing them age. These conversations, while challenging, build trust and understanding.

If your ageing loved one has memory issues or cognitive decline, these deeper conversations may need to take a different form. You might find yourself needing to process your emotions with someone else in your support network – a sibling, friend, counsellor or support group who understands your situation. This doesn't mean you can't connect meaningfully with your ageing loved one who has memory challenges. Rather, it acknowledges that your emotional processing might need additional outlets, while your connection with them focuses on present-moment experiences that don't rely heavily on memory.

Level 5 is the deepest and involves complete openness and acceptance. It's where we can share our deepest thoughts, memories and emotions without fear of judgement. With our ageing loved ones, these precious moments might come unexpectedly – perhaps during a quiet moment through old photos, or during a routine task that suddenly opens to deeper sharing.

For those with ageing loved ones facing memory challenges, these Level 5 connections might look different but be equally profound – perhaps through music that triggers emotional recognition, or simply sitting together in comfortable silence, holding hands and exchanging smiles that communicate more than words ever could.

Finding the right level

The key isn't to always aim for Level 5 conversations. Each level serves its purpose, and sometimes a warm exchange of pleasantries is exactly what's needed. Being aware of these levels helps us to:

- recognise opportunities to deepen connection when appropriate
- understand why some interactions feel more meaningful than others

- choose intentionally how to engage based on the situation and energy available.

Think about your recent conversations with your ageing loved one. Which level do you typically reach? Are you comfortable moving between levels? Sometimes, the most meaningful connections happen when we naturally flow between levels – starting with weather chat while making a cuppa, moving to family updates, sharing opinions about changes coming up, and perhaps reaching those deeper levels of personal feelings and peak communication.

Remember that different people have different comfort levels with emotional depth. Some of our ageing loved ones might not be comfortable expressing feelings openly. The goal isn't to force deeper conversations but to create safe spaces where they can naturally emerge.

To create opportunities for deeper connection:

- use physical objects, such as photos or mementos, to move conversations to deeper levels
- share your own feelings and experiences to create safety for deeper sharing
- pay attention to moments when your ageing loved one hints at deeper thoughts or emotions
- allow silence and space for reflection between sharing.

Remember that sometimes the deepest connections happen during the ordinary moments.

Becoming a masterful communicator

Communicating masterfully doesn't mean writing out a speech and reading it, practising your lines in the mirror or answering every question with another question. We're not turning every conversation into a contemplation of the sliding doors of life, the moments of disaster and disappointment, or a discussion of funeral prep. Pick something funny.

Masterful communication involves dancing between topics with grace, knowing when to lean in and when to step back, when to ask deeper questions and when to simply listen. Finding a comfortable rhythm means silences are as valuable as words, and both light and serious conversations have their place. You might say to your loved one, "I'm curious about what that was like for you," or, "Tell me more about how you felt then," rather than simply, "How are you?"

You'll find yourself naturally weaving questions about the past with present observations, creating bridges between memories and current moments. Some conversations gently reveal deeper

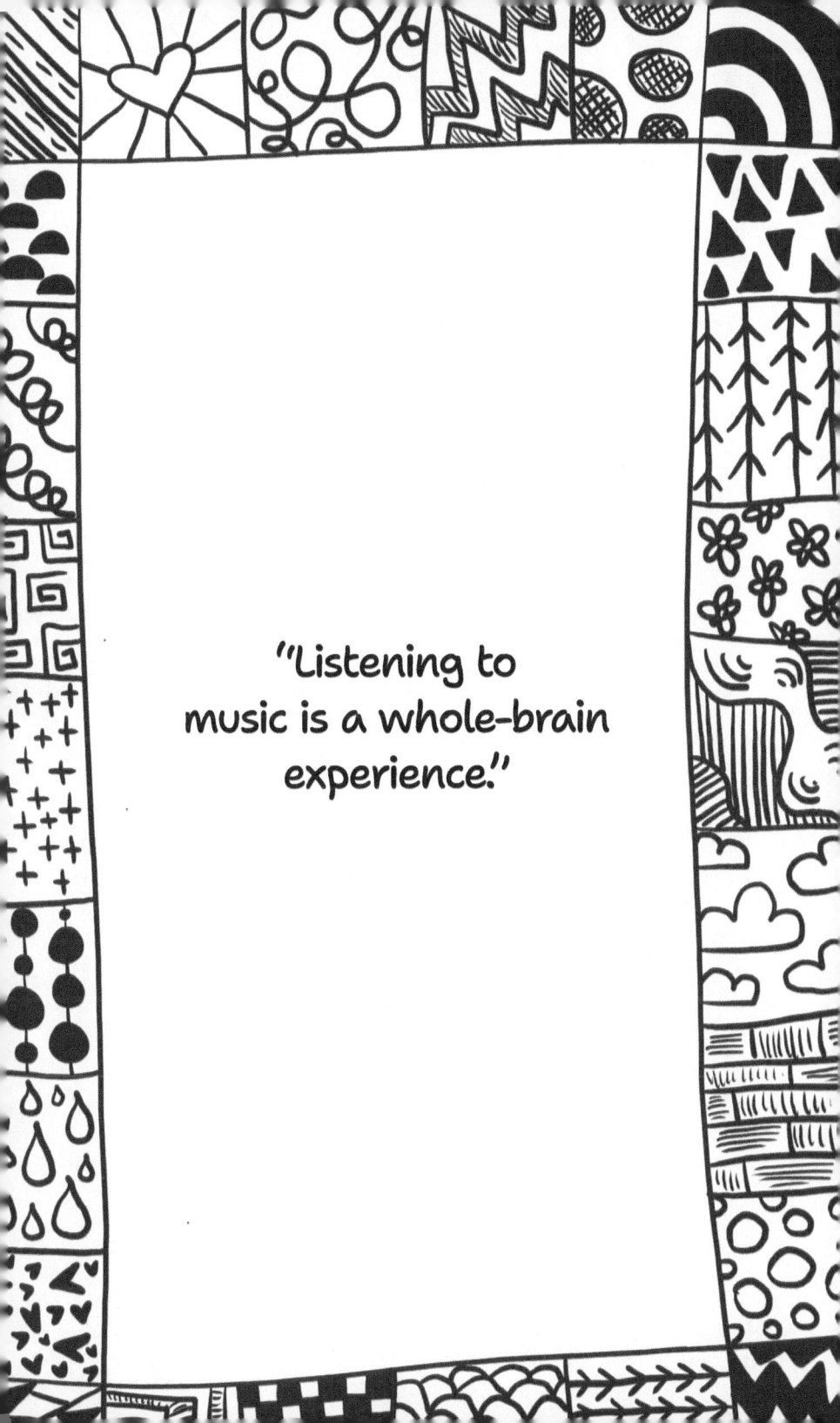

"Listening to music is a whole-brain experience."

layers of understanding, while others stay simple but meaningful. You'll notice both you and your loved one becoming more comfortable sharing thoughts and feelings, even during everyday tasks like preparing meals or sorting medications.

You might be thinking, *I feel awkward trying new communication approaches because it seems forced and unnatural*, or, *when I try to go deeper, my loved one changes the subject or withdraws, or our interactions are rushed or interrupted. I'm afraid of saying the wrong thing or triggering difficult emotions. All past attempts at meaningful conversation have led to conflict.* Like learning any new skill, advanced communication becomes natural with practice. Start small, celebrate progress and build from there.

When ageing loved ones seem uninterested, they're often protecting themselves from vulnerability or confusion. What looks like resistance is usually about feeling safe. Conversations need the right conditions to unfold. Start with light topics during familiar activities, and share your own stories first. Just as children often talk more openly in the car, older adults may open up when the pressure's off. One daughter found her quiet mother shared rich memories while they folded laundry; she just needed the right moment and setting.

The power of being present

You've just unlocked the difference between going through the motions and creating moments that matter. Your backpack is now full of strategies that transform everyday interactions into opportunities for genuine connection. You now understand how shifting your mindset changes everything. Routine tasks are no longer just items on your to-do list. The daily medication sorting is a chance for storytelling. The drive to the doctor is an opportunity for deeper understanding.

You've discovered the power of being present over being perfect, and you know how to dance between light conversations and meaningful dialogue. You can use humour as one of your most powerful connection tools. Laughter creates bonds that transcend age and circumstance. That shared chuckle over a familiar family story, the inside joke that only the two of you understand, or even finding something to smile about during challenging moments – these all create emotional bridges that words alone cannot build.

Don't underestimate humour's ability to diffuse tension, create warmth and make difficult conversations more approachable. Sometimes, the most meaningful connections happen not during serious heart-to-hearts but in the moments when you're both wiping away tears of laughter.

"Connection is where we find meaning ... as humans, our brains want to look for patterns ... we are pattern finders and pattern makers."

Hayley Langsdorf

You're now equipped to turn ordinary moments into extraordinary memories, one interaction at a time. You're not just caring for your ageing loved one anymore; you're connecting with them in ways that enrich both your lives and create lasting impressions that you'll treasure for years to come.

Mastering connection is an ongoing process. Each interaction builds on the previous ones and creates that tapestry of relationship and meaning. Stop expecting to master connection quickly. Start trying to deepen your communication with your ageing loved one. Your commitment to deepening connection with your ageing loved one isn't just about today; it's about creating a legacy of love and understanding that will impact generations to come.

Conclusion

THE SEEDS OF TOMORROW'S MEMORIES

As you reach these final pages, take a moment to reflect on the journey we've shared. You've discovered that meaningful connection with your ageing loved ones doesn't require grand gestures or endless time – it simply needs your intentional focus and presence.

You now have practical tools to create precious moments of connection, even within your busy schedule. Small actions, taken consistently, build into a tapestry of memories that both you and your loved one will treasure.

Picture yourself feeling confident and prepared in your role, knowing exactly how to make the most of your time together. Instead of being overwhelmed by tasks, you're creating natural opportunities for connection – whether it's sharing a cup of tea, looking through old photos or simply sitting together in comfortable silence.

Remember the key principles we've explored. Start small. Stay consistent. Be present. Focus on quality over quantity. These simple yet powerful guidelines will help you navigate this chapter of life with grace and purpose.

When the daily demands of life threaten to overshadow your intention to connect, return to the basics – even five minutes of focused attention can strengthen your bond and create a meaningful moment.

As you close this book, know that you have everything you need to create those precious moments of connection. Every small step you take today plants the seeds of tomorrow's memories.

May your journey be filled with meaningful moments that bring joy to both you and your ageing loved one. May we all find ways to make every moment matter in our relationships with those we hold dear.

Take action today

1. Choose one small connection strategy from this book and implement it this week.
2. Visit **connectionwithlana.com** now to download your free Connection Starter Kit, including the seven-day challenge calendar and reflection templates.
3. Share what you've learned with someone else caring for an ageing loved one – connection grows when we support each other.

This is your connection journey. Every small step you take today creates the memories you'll cherish tomorrow.

I invite you to join me in changing how we approach connection with our ageing loved ones. Visit my website to access additional resources and become part of our community of people committed to creating deeper connections and reducing future regrets.

The time to connect is now. Your ageing loved ones need your presence more than perfection, your attention more than achievement.

Let's reimagine connection with our ageing loved ones!

Lana

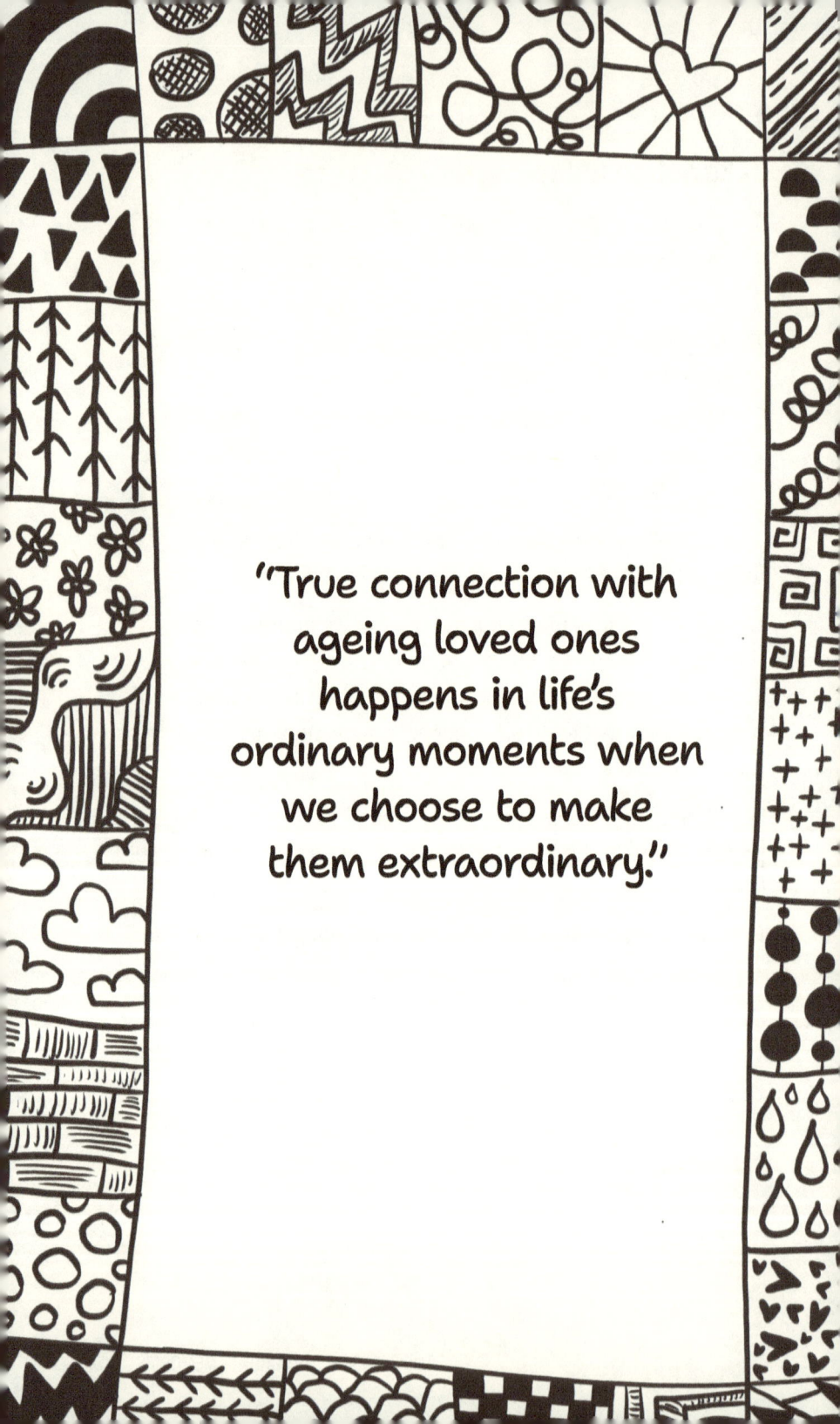

"True connection with ageing loved ones happens in life's ordinary moments when we choose to make them extraordinary."

www.ingramcontent.com/pod-product-compliance
Lightning Source LLC
Chambersburg PA
CBHW030328080526
44584CB00012B/763

Freeing Unconditional Love

What people are saying about Freeing Unconditional Love: Unchaining Your True Self!

Susan Marion speaks from her heart! *Freeing Unconditional Love: Unchaining Your True Self!* is a MUST read for everyone! Her in-depth discussion of all those little [or big] head voices everyone has is enlightening, inspiring, and motivating. Her "system" for healing yourself from the inside out is so easy anyone can do it. The best part is that once you put this system to use for yourself, you will reap benefits beyond anything you might have anticipated. Your life will bee more joyous, healthy and free. Susan's book offers the reader a chance for personal freedom; a chance to break from the limiting parameters so many of us have erected around our minds, hearts, souls and lives. My recommendation: READ IT NOW! and then put the action steps into place in YOUR life, step back and watch what happens! Enjoy!

Barbara Legan, The Life Mentor,
www.thelifementor.com
Sedona, AZ.

Susan brings a feeling of renewal, even if in that renewal we must go through the pain, it's what most of us hide and she lays it all on the line in an honest and genuine way which is not overlooked by a sincere heart. I relate to that, people relate to that. Books like this open portholes of thought. Thought that easily brings in the light of a shared perspective or understanding that can CHANGE lives. This book made me want to uncover my own demons of childhood and look them square in the eye for how they might impede my adult progress and limit my potential.

Mona McPherson.
Palm Coast, Florida

Susan Ann Marion

For the first time in maybe forever, I am going to be and relishing the thought of what my new "companion" may discover tomorrow… I know, not free yet, or whole, but I am soooo much better than yesterday or the day before. Susan gave me a tool that might possibly have given me a new lease on life. Thank you, thank you, thank you.

Paula Kiwala
Bunnell, Florida